The Industrial

MW00774161

The industrialization of prostitution and the sex trade has created a multibillion-dollar global market, involving millions of women, that makes a substantial contribution to national and global economies.

The Industrial Vagina examines how prostitution and other aspects of the sex industry have moved from being small-scale, clandestine and socially despised practices to become very profitable legitimate market sectors that are being legalized and decriminalized by governments. Sheila Jeffreys demonstrates how prostitution has been globalized through an examination of:

- the growth of pornography and its new global reach
- the boom in adult shops, strip clubs and escort agencies
- military prostitution and sexual violence in war
- marriage and the mail order bride industry
- the rise in sex tourism and trafficking in women

She argues that through these practices women's subordination has been outsourced and that states that legalize this industry are acting as pimps, enabling male buyers in countries in which women's equality threatens male dominance to buy access to the bodies of women from poor countries who are paid for their sexual subservience.

This major and provocative contribution is essential reading for all with an interest in feminist, gender and critical globalization issues as well as students and scholars of international political economy.

Sheila Jeffreys is a Professor in the School of Social and Political Sciences at the University of Melbourne. She is the author of six other books on the history and politics of sexuality, including *Beauty and Misogyny* (Routledge, 2005). She is the founding member of the Australian branch of the Coalition Against Trafficking in Women.

RIPE Series in Global Political Economy

This series, published in association with the *Review of International Political Economy*, provides a forum for current and interdisciplinary debates in international political economy. The series aims to advance understanding of the key issues in the global political economy, and to present innovative analyses of emerging topics. The titles in the series focus on three broad themes:

- the structures, processes and actors of contemporary global transformations
- the changing forms taken by governance, at scales from the local and everyday to the global and systemic
- the inseparability of economic from political, social and cultural questions, including resistance, dissent and social movements.

The series comprises two strands:

The *RIPE Series in Global Political Economy* aims to address the needs of students and teachers, and the titles will be published in hardback and paperback. Titles include

Transnational Classes and International Relations
Kees van der Pijl

Gender and Global Restructuring:
Sightings, Sites and Resistances
Edited by Marianne H Marchand and Anne Sisson Runyan

Global Political Economy
Contemporary Theories
Edited by Ronen Palan

Ideologies of Globalization
Contending Visions of a New World Order
Mark Rupert

The Clash within Civilisations
Coming to Terms with Cultural Conflicts
Dieter Senghaas

Global Unions?
Theory and Strategies of Organized Labour in the Global
Political Economy
Edited by Jeffrey Harrod and Robert O'Brien

Political Economy of a Plural World
Critical Reflections on Power, Morals and Civilizations
Robert Cox with Michael Schechter

A Critical Rewriting of Global Political Economy
Integrating Reproductive, Productive and Virtual Economies
V. Spike Peterson

Contesting Globalization
Space and Place in the World Economy
André C. Drainville

Global Institutions and Development
Framing the World?
Edited by Morten Bøås and Desmond McNeill

Global Institutions, Marginalization, and Development
Craig N. Murphy

Critical Theories, International Relations and 'the Anti-Globalisation Movement'
The Politics of Global Resistance
Edited by Catherine Eschle and Bice Maiguashca

Globalization, Governmentality, and Global Politics
Regulation for the Rest of Us?
Ronnie D. Lipschutz, with James K. Rowe

Critical Perspectives on Global Governance
Rights and Regulation in Governing Regimes
Jean Grugel and Nicola Piper

Beyond States and Markets
The Challenges of Social Reproduction
Edited by Isabella Bakker and Rachel Silvey

The Industrial Vagina
The Political Economy of the Global Sex Trade
Sheila Jeffreys

Routledge/RIPE Studies in Global Political Economy is a forum for innovative new research intended for a high-level specialist readership, and the titles will be available in hardback only. Titles include:

1. Globalization and Governance*
Edited by Aseem Prakash and Jeffrey A. Hart

2. Nation-States and Money
The Past, Present and Future of National Currencies
Edited by Emily Gilbert and Eric Helleiner

3. The Global Political Economy of Intellectual Property Rights
The New Enclosures?
Christopher May

4. Integrating Central Europe
EU Expansion and Poland, Hungary and the Czech Republic
Otto Holman

5. Capitalist Restructuring, Globalization and the Third Way
Lessons from the Swedish Model
J. Magnus Ryner

Praise for previous publications

By Sheila Jeffreys

BEAUTY AND MISOGYNY: HARMFUL CULTURAL PRACTICES IN THE WEST (ROUTLEDGE: 2005)

If readers are prepared to see the glitzy world of beauty through Sheila Jeffreys' eyes a whole new picture becomes available that is far from beautiful and which involves a re-evaluation of the meaning of beauty practices on a personal as well as a societal level. *Beauty and Misogyny* is not bedtime reading, but rather a brilliantly written, yet hard to digest, analysis of everyday realities that too often slip out of critical review by academic scholars and everyday women. It unmasks 'beauty' as a 'bastion of male dominance' (p. 197) that needs to be breached if these achievements are to be made towards the equal status of women. To conquer this bastion, however, women need to be aware of the roots and consequences of beauty practices. This process of consciousness-raising is central to Jeffreys' analysis and makes this book such an important one in a time where it all seems to come down to women's 'personal choice'.

Nadine Zacharias, University of Ballarat,
in *The Melbourne Journal of Politics*, January 2006

Sheila Jeffreys' book represents a powerful and provocative response to both liberal and postmodern feminists' defence of beauty practices against earlier feminist critiques of the 1960s and 1970s ... Overall, this book is passionately and persuasively argued and the examples given lend weight to Jeffreys' position, particularly in the concluding chapters ... Jeffreys writes with wit, clarity and vigour and her book is essential reading for feminist scholars and researchers.

Jo Pike, University of Hull, in *Feminist Theory*, 2006, 7: 366

In Jeffreys' latest book, she questions why the beauty industry is expanding, and why liberal feminists should see a virtue in women having the power to choose practices that a few years back were condemned as oppressive. The critique of beauty practices, written about by Dworkin in *Woman Hating*, in 1974, has today all but disappeared, making way for procedures that 'break skin and spill blood' ... The book is one she has wanted to write for years, as 'liberal feminists and postmodernists' challenge the early feminist critique of beauty practices. 'Not only are the practices creeping back, they are becoming more severe and invasive of the body itself,' she says ... Jeffreys offers no comfort zone for her readers. Unlike some feminist theorists, she refuses to couch her arguments in inaccessible, academic language, or to accept that feminism has achieved its aims. For Jeffreys, the word 'complicated' does not exist. The reason for women's oppression is horribly simple: men want their power and, for that reason, they will keep women in a state of subordination to maintain it.

Julie Bindel, *Guardian*, 2005

The Industrial Vagina

The political economy of the global sex trade

Sheila Jeffreys

Routledge
Taylor & Francis Group

LONDON AND NEW YORK

First published 2009
by Routledge
2 Park Square, Milton Park, Abingdon, Oxon OX14 4RN

Simultaneously published in the USA and Canada
by Routledge
270 Madison Ave, New York, NY 10016

Reprinted 2009 (twice)

Transferred to Digital Printing 2009

*Routledge is an imprint of the Taylor & Francis Group,
an informa business*

© 2009 Sheila Jeffreys

Typeset in Sabon by Keyword Group Ltd
Printed and bound in Great Britain by
TJI Digital, Padstow, Cornwall

British Library Cataloguing in Publication Data
A catalogue record for this book is available
from the British Library

Library of Congress Cataloging in Publication Data
Jeffreys, Sheila.
   The industrial vagina : the political economy of the
   global sex trade / Sheila Jeffreys.
      p. cm.
   Includes bibliographical references.
   ISBN 978-0-415-41232-2 (hardback) –
   ISBN 978-0-415-41233-9 (pbk.) –
   ISBN 978-0-203-69830-3 (ebook)
   1. Prostitution–Political aspects. 2. Prostitution–
   Economic aspects. 3. Prostitution–Social aspects.
   4. Sex-oriented businesses. 5. Feminism. I. Title.
HQ117.J45 2008
306.74'2–dc22   2008021869

ISBN10: 0-415-41232-2 (hbk)
ISBN10: 0-415-41233-1 (pbk)
ISBN10: 0-203-69830-4 (ebk)

ISBN13: 978-0-415-41232-2 (hbk)
ISBN13: 978-0-415-41233-9 (pbk)
ISBN13: 978-0-203-69830-3 (ebk)

I dedicate this book to my partner, Ann Rowett, for the love and strength she has given me during the writing of this book. It is also dedicated to all my sisters in the international struggle to end men's prostitution of women. In particular women in the CATW network in the US, in Europe, in the Philippines and in Australia, such as Janice G. Raymond, Malka Marcovich, Jean Enriquez, Aurora Javarte de Dios, Gunilla Ekberg, and many others who have inspired and encouraged my work. They have made me feel part of something extraordinary, an international uprising of women against this traditional injustice.

Contents

Introduction
From pimping to a profitable market sector

Prostitution did not wither away. Despite the confident understandings of feminists before the 1980s that prostitution was a sign and example of women's subordination which would cease to exist when women gained equality, at the end of the 20th century it had been constructed into a burgeoning and immensely profitable global market sector. This development is surprising if we consider the ways in which prostitution has been regarded by feminists over two centuries to be the very model of women's subordination (Jeffreys, 1985a). Kate Millett wrote in 1970 that prostitution was, 'paradigmatic, somehow the very core of the female's condition' which reduced woman to 'cunt' (Millett, 1975, p. 56). Feminists in the 1960s and 1970s understood prostitution to be a hangover from traditional male dominant societies that would disappear with the advance of women's equality. It was, as Millett put it, a 'living fossil', an old form of slave relations still existing in the present (ibid.). However, in the late 20th century various forces came together to breathe new life into this 'harmful cultural practice' (Jeffreys, 2004). The most important is the new economic ideology and practice of these times, neo-liberalism, in which the tolerance of 'sexual freedom' has been merged with a free market ideology to reconstruct prostitution as legitimate 'work' which can form the basis of national and international sex industries. This book analyses the processes by which prostitution has been industrialized and globalized in the late 20th and early 21st century. It argues that this growing market sector needs to be understood as the commercialization of women's subordination, and suggests how the rolling back of the global sex industry can begin.

Until the 1970s there was consensus amongst state governments and in international law that prostitution should not be legalized or organized by states. This consensus followed a successful international campaign by women's groups and others against state regulation of prostitution from the late 19th century onwards (Jeffreys, 1997). This intensified through the League of Nations committee on trafficking in persons between the two world wars and culminated in the 1949 Convention on Trafficking in Persons and Exploitation of the Prostitution of Others. This Convention identified prostitution in its preamble as incompatible with the dignity and worth of the human person. It outlawed brothel keeping. In response to the Convention and the zeitgeist that it represented, pimping, living off the earnings of prostitution and procuring for prostitution were outlawed both in states which had signed up to this convention and in those which had not.

This mood of universal condemnation changed in the neo-liberal 1980s and the process began by which pimps were transformed into respectable business people who could join the Rotary Club. The business of brothel prostitution was legalized and turned into a 'market sector' in countries like Australia, the Netherlands, Germany and New Zealand, stripping became a regular part of the 'leisure' or 'entertainment' industry, and pornography became respectable enough for corporations like General Motors to make porn channels part of their stable. Whilst a section of the industry of prostitution became legal, respectable and a profitable market sector in this period, the vast majority of prostitution both within those western countries that legalized and throughout the world remained illegal and a most profitable sector for organized crime.

This book will look at practices in which cash or goods are exchanged in order for men to obtain sexual access to the bodies of girls and women. I include those practices generally recognized as prostitution in which men, through payment or the offer of some other advantage, gain the right to use their hands, penises, mouths or objects on or in the bodies of women. Though the prostitution of boys and young men for the sexual use of other men is a small part of this industry, this will not be considered in detail here (see Jeffreys, 1997). Included within this definition are the forms of marriage practice in which girls and women are exchanged between patriarchal families with the exchange of cash or favours, including child marriage and forced marriage, or through payment to agencies as in the case of the mail order bride industry. Pornography is included because it is different from other forms of prostitution only because it is filmed. It involves payment to girls and women for sexual access.

Stripping is included not just because prostitution and lap dancing take place in the clubs, but because it involves the sexual use of women even when no touching takes place. The practices covered here fit into the concept of 'sexual exploitation' which is the subject of the 1991 Draft UN Convention Against Sexual Exploitation: 'Sexual exploitation is a practice by which person(s) achieve sexual gratification, or financial gain, or advancement, through the abuse of a person's sexuality by abrogating that person's human right to dignity, equality, autonomy, and physical and mental wellbeing' (for discussion of this Draft Convention and the text, see Defeis, 2000). 'Sexual exploitation' includes non-pecuniary practices such as rape, whereas this book looks at commercial sexual exploitation in which the main means of power employed to extract sexual access from girls and women is economic, though other forms such as brutal force, kidnap and deceit may also be involved.

The industrialization and globalization of prostitution

This book will show that, in recent decades, prostitution has been industrialized and globalized. By industrialization I mean the ways in which traditional forms of organization of prostitution are being changed by economic and social forces to become large scale and concentrated, normalized and part of the mainstream corporate sphere. Prostitution has been transformed from an illegal, small-scale, largely local and socially despised form of abuse of women into a hugely profitable and either legal or tolerated international industry. In states that have legalized their prostitution industries large-scale, industrialized brothels employ hundreds of women overseen and regulated by government agencies (M. Sullivan, 2007). In some parts of Asia the industrialization of prostitution has taken place in the form of the creation of massive prostitution areas within cities. In Daulatdia, formed 20 years ago, in a port city in Bangladesh, 1,600 women are sexually used by 3,000 men daily (Hammond, 2008). This book will look at the globalization of prostitution too, examining the ways in which the global sex industry has been integrated into the international political economy. Kathleen Barry explains that, since 1970, 'the most dramatic changes in prostitution have been its industrialization, normalization, and widespread global diffusion' (Barry, 1995, p. 122). The result of the industrialization has been 'a multibillion-dollar global market in women, at home and abroad, in highly organized trafficking and in the most diffused, informal arrangements' (ibid.). A 1998 International Labour Organization (ILO) report supplies powerful evidence to suggest that prostitution was organized on a quite new scale and integrated into national economies in significant ways in the 1990s. As Lin Leam Lim comments:

> Prostitution has changed recently in some SE Asian countries. The scale of prostitution has been enlarged to an extent where we can justifiably speak of a commercial sex sector that is integrated into the economic, social and political life of these countries. The sex business has assumed the dimensions of an industry and has directly or indirectly contributed in no small measure to employment, national income and economic growth.
>
> (Lim, 1998, p. vi)

The report is broadly positive about this development as good for the economies of these countries, arguing that prostitution should be recognized as legitimate by governments because of its profitability, even if they do not go so far as to legalize it.

Prostitution is now a significant market sector within national economies, though the worth of domestic sex industries is hard to estimate, considering the size of the illegal industry and the general lack of transparency that surrounds it. The industry of prostitution is most developed and entrenched in those countries in which militaries such as the US and Japan in the 1930s and 1940s set up prostitution systems on a scale and with a precision which is industrial, such as Korea, the Philippines and Thailand (Moon, 1997; Tanaka, 2002). The ILO report estimated that the sex industry accounts for 2–14 per cent of the worth of economies in the four countries studied, the Philippines, Malaysia, Thailand and Indonesia (ibid.). The Korean government estimated in 2002 that one million women were in prostitution at any one time in the country (Hurt, 2005). The industry was estimated to be worth 4.4 per cent of gross domestic product (GDP), more than forestry, fishing and agriculture combined (4.1 per cent). This was said to be a conservative estimate since many forms of prostitution were untrackable. It was estimated that between 1 in 6 and 1 in 10 of women in the country have worked in some capacity in prostitution (ibid.). The sex industry in the Netherlands, which legalized brothel prostitution in 2001, has been estimated to be worth 5 per cent of GDP (Daley, 2001). In China the boom in the prostitution industry since the move towards a market economy from 1978 onwards has been particularly notable since it has developed from a low base in the Maoist era when prostitution was not tolerated. There are now an estimated 200,000–300,000 prostituted women in Beijing alone and anywhere between 10 and 20 million prostituted women in China as a whole (Zhou, 2006). The industry of prostitution is estimated to account for 8 per cent of the Chinese economy, and to be worth about US$700 billion (ibid.).

The globalization of the sex industry is embedding prostitution in the international economy in many ways. The trafficking of women has become valuable to national economies, for instance, because of the remittances these women send to the home country. Governments like that of the Philippines have encouraged the trade by providing training for women before they leave. In 2004 Filipinas in Japan sent home $258 million. $8.5 billion in annual remittances from all Filipinos working abroad comprises 10 per cent of the country's income (McCurry, 2005, p. 15). Eighty thousand Filipinas entered Japan in 2004 on six-month entertainment visas, of whom up to 90 per cent were required to work in the sex industry. Globalization is enabling US pornography and strip club companies such as Spearmint Rhino and the Hustler chain, and the organized crime that is typically connected to them, to make profits from products and venues in many countries. Spearmint Rhino has a club in Melbourne. The US Hustler chain of Larry Flynt has acquired one too, and installed a local Melbourne pimp, Maxine Fensom, to run it. A celebratory article in the *Sunday Age* newspaper explains that Fensom is working with US 'adult' industry figures to create a home-grown Australian pornography industry based in Melbourne to make 'gonzo porn', which is the most debasing and abusive kind, for the American market, starting with 'Aussie f ... fest' (Halliday, 2007).

The sex industry does not just make profits for brothel and strip club owners and newly respectable pornography companies. Many other actors benefit economically, which helps to embed prostitution within national economies (Poulin, 2005). Hotels and airlines benefit from sex tourism, and business sex tourism. Taxi drivers who deliver the male buyers to brothels and strip clubs are given rakeoffs from the sex industry for doing so. Others who benefit include the bouncers and valets at strip clubs, and the businesses that service strippers with costumes and makeup. They include the companies that market the alcoholic drinks that are consumed in those clubs. Two Scotch whisky companies, Chivas Regal and Johnnie Walker, have been identified as profiting from brothel prostitution in Thailand, for example, and thus, according to the Scottish *Daily Record*, fuelling the child prostitution and Asian crime barons that are so integral to the Thai industry (Lironi, 2005). Chivas Regal's 12 per cent profit growth in 2004 was attributed in one report to its association with Thai brothels. All of these profits are made from the sale of women's bodies in the marketplace, though the women themselves, as we shall see, are receiving a very small share of them.

The globalization of the sex industry means that markets in women's bodies are no longer confined within national boundaries. Trafficking, sex tourism and the mail order bride business have ensured that women's severe inequality can be transferred beyond national boundaries as the women of poor countries can be sexually bought by men from rich countries (Belleau, 2003). The late 20th century saw the wholesale engagement of prostitutors from rich countries in the prostitution of women from poor countries in a new form of sexual colonization. This is taking place through the mail order bride industry, in which women from Latin America are imported into the US, for instance, or women from the Philippines into Australia. It is taking place also through the industry of sex tourism. As part of tours organized through rich countries, or as individual 'tourists', rich buyers seek out local or trafficked women in sex tourism destinations. Thus men can be compensated for the loss of their status in countries where women have made strides towards equality, by outsourcing women's subordination to be consumed elsewhere or from imported poor women. The supply chain has been internationalized with large-scale trafficking of women from poor countries on every continent into destinations which include their richer neighbours, i.e. from North Korea to China, and to western sex tourism destinations such as Germany and the Netherlands. The Internet offers male buyers in the US sex chat lines funnelled through impoverished island states (Lane, 2001). This integration of the sex industry into global capitalism has not been sufficiently remarked or studied, and the implications for women's status and for governance have scarcely been remarked at all.

New technologies such as air travel have facilitated movement of prostituted women and girls and of the buyers and thus increased the scale and international scope of the industry. Similarly the Internet has enabled sex tourism, the mail order bride business and other forms of prostitution to expand and interrelate. New electronic technologies from the videotape to the Internet have enabled the development of a massively profitable industry with a global reach, in which women in poor countries can be delivered in film or in real time to perform sex acts for men in the west (Hughes, 1999). Though the technologies which enable women's bodies to be delivered to male buyers change and develop, the vagina and the other parts of women's bodies which form the raw material of prostitution remain resolutely 'old technology' and impervious to change. The vagina becomes the centre of a business organized on an industrial scale though the vagina itself is still subject to the problems inevitably associated with the use of the interior of a woman's body in this way, in the form of pain, bleeding and abrasion, pregnancy and sexually transmitted disease, and the associated psychological harms that result from the bodies of live women being used as instruments of men's pleasure.

Prostitution is being globalized too through the process of economic development in countries previously organized around subsistence. Prostitution, or in some cases particular forms of prostitution, is exported to the sites of industrial development in 'poor' countries such as Papua New Guinea and the Solomon Islands (Wardlow, 2007; UNESCAP, 2007). Thus as foreign mining and logging companies open up new areas for new forms of colonial exploitation they set up prostitution industries to service the workers. These industries have a profound effect on local cultures and relations between men and women. This practice has a history in the 'development' of Australia in the 19th century, for instance, when aboriginal women or trafficked Japanese women were employed to service men involved in taking over indigenous lands for mining and cattle farming (Frances, 2007).

Traditional international politics does not include the sex industry within its concerns, as indeed it does not consider many other issues that relate to women and girls. Feminist theorists have advanced considerably in the last ten years in the gendering of international politics and international relations in particular. Cynthia Enloe was a pioneer in making prostitution a concern for feminist international politics through her work on militarism and military prostitution in the 1980s (Enloe, 1983, 1989). More recently feminist international politics texts have covered the issues of the trafficking in women and sex tourism, notably the work of Jan Pettman (Pettman, 1996). But feminist work on the international political economy has generally either omitted prostitution or included it in ways which are problematic, i.e. as a form of reproductive and 'socially necessary' labour (Peterson, 2003). Trafficking in women has been the subject of a great outpouring of research in the last decade (Farr, 2004; Monzini, 2005), but other aspects of the industry such as pornography, for instance, have not been looked at in an international perspective. The only book which looks at the global sex industry as a whole from a political economy perspective is Richard Poulin's very useful *La Mondialisation des industries du sexe* (2005).

Language matters

In the last two decades the language used in academic literature and in policy formation has changed considerably as prostitution has been normalized. Even feminist scholars and activists now generally use a new euphemistic language, such that it has become unusual to find 'prostitution' referred to at all. In consonance with the understanding promoted by some sex work advocacy groups in the 1980s, prostitution is commonly referred to currently as 'sex work', which suggests that it should be seen as a legitimate form of work (Jeffreys, 1997; Jeness, 1993). Those who promote the notion that prostitution should be seen as ordinary work I shall refer to as the 'sex work lobby' and the ideas that underlie this approach as the 'sex work position'. The sex work position is the basis of the demands for the normalization and legalization of prostitution. As a corollary of this position the men who buy women are now commonly referred to as 'clients', which normalizes their practice as just another form of consumer activity. Those who run prostitution venues and take the profits from the industry are regularly referred to in my state of Victoria, Australia, where brothels are regulated by the Business Licensing Authority, as 'service providers' (M. Sullivan, 2007).

In the 1990s the language relating to the trafficking of women into prostitution has also been changed by those who consider prostitution an ordinary market sector. Thus trafficking is now called, by many sex worker activists and those in migration studies, migration for labour (Agustin, 2006a). Language is important. The use of the ordinary language of commerce in relation to prostitution makes the harm of this practice invisible. It facilitates the profitable development of the global industry. If any progress is to be made in reining in the global industry then language which makes the harm visible must be retained or developed. In this book I use language which calls attention to the harm that prostitution constitutes for women. Thus I refer to prostituted women rather than sex workers, because this suggests that something harmful is being done to the women and brings the perpetrators into the picture. I call the male buyers 'prostitutors', rather than clients, in reference to the useful word in Spanish 'prostituidor', i.e. the man who prostitutes the woman, a formulation that suggests disapproval and one that is not available in English. I refer to those who gain third party profits as pimps and procurers, terms which may now seem old-fashioned but which show a reasonable disdain for the practice of deriving profits from women's pain. States which legalize their prostitution industries I refer to as 'pimp states'. I shall continue to use the term 'trafficking in women' to refer to the practice of transporting women into debt bondage.

Prostitution as a harmful cultural practice

Most of the academic and feminist literature on prostitution which uses the language of 'sex work' is based upon the premise that it is possible, or even desirable, to make distinctions between various forms of the sex industry; between child and adult prostitution, between trafficking and prostitution, between forced and free trafficking, between forced and free prostitution, between legal and illegal sectors of the industry, between prostitution in the west and prostitution in the non-west. The creation of distinctions legitimizes forms of prostitution by criticizing some and not others. This book is different because it looks for connections and interrelationships rather than distinctions. It looks at the ways in which all these aspects of sexual exploitation depend upon and involve one another. Those who seek to make distinctions generally subscribe to the notion that there is a free and respectable kind of prostitution for adults which can be seen as ordinary work and legalized, a form of prostitution for the rational, choosing individual, based upon equality and contract. The vast majority of prostitution fits this image very badly indeed but it is the necessary fiction that underlies the normalization and legalization of the industry.

This book employs a radical feminist framework which understands prostitution to be a harmful cultural practice originating in the subordination of women (Jeffreys, 2004) and constituting a form of violence against women (Jeffreys, 1997). It is inspired by the work of other radical feminist theorists on prostitution such as Kathleen Barry (1979, 1995) and Andrea Dworkin (1983), and seeks to extend their analyses to the global industry in a variety of its forms. Since this book takes the perspective that prostitution is harmful to women it does not take a normalizing approach. Thus the book ends with a consideration of ways in which the global industry of prostitution may best be wound back, so that the traditional feminist hopefulness of ending prostitution may once more become imaginable and a reasonable goal for feminists to pursue in public policy.

The Industrial Vagina starts from the understanding that prostitution is a harmful cultural practice. It is overwhelmingly a practice that is carried out through and in the bodies of women and for the benefit of men. Since the 1970s there has been considerable development in the recognition of what are called in United Nations documents 'Harmful traditional/cultural practices' (Jeffreys, 2005). The words traditional and cultural are used interchangeably in UN literature on this subject. This development is the result of feminist campaigning and was kickstarted by concerns about female genital mutilation, which can be considered the paradigmatic 'harmful cultural practice'. This concern was written into the 1979 United Nations Convention on the Elimination of all Forms of Discrimination Against Women (CEDAW). Article 2(f) of CEDAW states that parties to the Convention will 'take all appropriate measures, including legislation, to modify or abolish existing laws, regulations, *customs and practices* which constitute discrimination against women' (my italics). Article 5(a) similarly states that 'all appropriate measures' will be taken to 'modify *the social and cultural patterns of conduct* of men and women, with a view to achieving the elimination of prejudices and *customary* and all other practices which are based on the idea of the inferiority or the superiority of either of the sexes or on stereotyped roles for men and women' (my italics). Prostitution fits these criteria particularly well. It stems from the understanding that women have the stereotyped role of providing their bodies for men's pleasure with no concern for their feelings or personhood. In the case of the prostitutors it encompasses the stereotyped role of men acting out their patriarchal right to use the bodies of women who wish to be elsewhere, or may even be crying from the pain, for their own satisfaction. It is justified by tradition as in the frequently uttered nostrum that it is the 'oldest profession'. Slavery is old too but seldom justified by its longevity. The feminist historian Gerda Lerner writes most usefully about the way in which brothel prostitution in the ancient Middle East originated in the enslavement of captives in warfare, as a way of tidily dealing with surplus women slaves (Lerner, 1987).

The definition of harmful traditional practices was extended in 1995 in a UN Fact Sheet No. 23 entitled *Harmful Traditional Practices Affecting the Health of Women and Children*. The criteria offered in the introduction cover several aspects which fit prostitution very well. The practices damage the health of women and girls, and there is a wealth of accumulating evidence about the extent of the harm that prostitution wreaks on health (Farley, 2004). Traditional cultural practices are said to 'reflect values and beliefs held by members of a community for periods often spanning generations' and are said to persist because they are not questioned and take on an aura of morality in the eyes of those practising them (United Nations, 1995, pp. 3–4). Though many values and beliefs of male dominance have been or are in the process of change in many societies, the idea that prostitution is necessary, as a way of protecting non-prostituted women from assault for instance, or because men cannot control themselves, is actually gaining in strength rather than diminishing. The practices are 'performed for male benefit', and it would be hard to argue that prostitution was not to men's benefit considering who is harmed thereby (ibid.). They are 'consequences of the value placed on women and the girl child by society', and they 'persist in an environment where women and the girl child have unequal access to education, wealth, health and employment'.

Many of the harmful cultural practices recognized in the international human rights community originate in the exchange of women. The exchange of women between men for the purpose of sexual and reproductive access and to extract free labour is the foundation of the subordination of women, and still deeply rooted within patriarchal cultures (Rubin, 1975). It can take a variety of forms, of which prostitution as commonly encountered in western cities is but one. Other forms of exchange in which the power relations of male dominance are clear, such as forms of marriage involving children, bride price and dowry, force or cultural pressure rather than free choice, temporary marriage and concubinage, are all fairly well understood to be harmful cultural practices based upon women's subordination. But, as we shall see in this book, prostitution is integrally bound up with all of these other practices that have related origins. Women and girls are trafficked into brothel prostitution, but also into marriage and concubinage. It can be hard to separate out one of these practices from another. Prostitution is often seen as the opposite of marriage but, as we shall see in Chapter 2, there is in many cases barely a whisker of difference between these two dominant forms of patriarchal exchange of women. It is because prostitution is a harmful cultural practice that it cannot be airbrushed into a respectable industry. It is not like domestic labour, into which women are also trafficked and kept in servile conditions, though in considerably smaller numbers, because domestic labour can be done by men and is not necessarily based on women's biology and oppression. Domestic labour is not in itself a harmful cultural practice, though the conditions in which it is carried out can be profoundly harmful for women. This book is about the way in which this harmful cultural practice has been turned into a massively profitable global industry which is defended by proponents of the sex work position as the exercise of women's 'agency' and a form of 'entrepreneurship'.

The importance of social acceptance

The increasing profitability and expansion of the global sex industry depends on social acceptance. It requires that governments either tolerate or legalize the industry. Thus an industry report on the legalized brothel and strip club industry in Australia in 2007 makes it clear that increasing social acceptance is crucial to the continuing and increasing profits of the sex industry. A 'key success factor' listed in the report is 'ability to effectively change community behaviour' and this is necessary because of the 'significant level of moral stigma attached to prostitution' (IBISWorld, 2007, p. 22). The report notes that there has been a rise in 'consumer acceptance' but the industry is vulnerable to the 'negative image largely due to the moral, health and safety issues associated with it'. As the report puts it, 'entities are acutely sensitive to bad press that reduces the trust between (existing and potential) customers, the authorities and the general public' (IBISWorld, 2007, p. 8). Such a comment suggests that feminist and community opposition could be effective in containing the industry. Unfortunately the majority of academic and activist feminist writing on prostitution in the present normalizes prostitution in its language and in its central concepts. This development in feminist theory is examined and criticized in Chapter 1.

Feminists and the global sex industry

Cheerleaders or critics?

National sex industries and the global sex industry are currently experiencing startling growth and profit levels (IBISWorld, 2007; Poulin, 2005). In consonance, the many problems that are now being recognized as intrinsically linked to the industry, harms to the health of women and girls (Jeffreys, 2004), organized crime and corruption (M. Sullivan, 2007), trafficking (Farr, 2004; Monzini, 2005), the early sexualization of girls (American Psychological Association, 2007), are growing apace. It is surprising in this context that many theorists and researchers on prostitution who define themselves as feminists, or concern themselves primarily with the interests of women, are increasingly using euphemisms in their approach to prostitution. The language of feminist theorists on prostitution was affected by the normalization of the industry in the last decades of the 20th century. Though some remained critical (Barry, 1995; Jeffreys, 1997; Stark and Whisnant, 2004), many started to use a language more in tune with the neo-liberal economists, such as Milton Friedman, who were calling for the decriminalization of prostitution and its treatment just like any other industry. They began to use terms such as 'agency', 'entrepreneurship' and 'rational choice' to describe the experience of prostituted women. These approaches are a public relations victory for the international sex industry. In this chapter I shall critically analyse the neo-liberal language and ideas that many feminists have adopted to see whether they are suited to the new realities.

The main vectors of neo-liberal language in relation to prostitution are the sex work agencies set up or funded by governments to supply condoms to prostituted women and men against the transmission of HIV. This 'AIDS money' has created a powerful force of sex workers' rights organizations which take the position that prostitution is just a job like any other, and now a useful market sector that must be decriminalized. Leading propagandists of this movement argue that AIDS funding has been crucial to their success in pushing the decriminalization argument (Doezema, 1998b). The international umbrella grouping of these sex work organizations is the Network of Sex Work Projects (NSWP) which uses neo-liberal understandings of prostitution to coordinate the international campaign for decriminalization through the work of activists such as Laura Agustin (2004, 2006b), and Jo Doezema (1998b). Jo Doezema, an NSWP spokeswoman, argues that AIDS money gave a big impetus to the campaign. She says: 'The original impetus for the NSWP came from the huge amount of interest in sex workers due to the AIDS pandemic. Vast amounts of resources were pumped into projects and research to stop sex workers from spreading AIDS' (Murphy and Ringheim, n.d.). Kamala Kempadoo, a significant researcher in the area of sex tourism and prostitution in the Caribbean who takes a sex work position, echoes the importance of AIDS money: 'some AIDS-prevention work has contributed to the formation of new sex worker organizations, inadvertently empowering sex workers in other areas than just in health matters' (Kempadoo, 1998, p. 19).

With the advent of AIDS funding, sex worker activists gained platforms and an authority, as experts in a supposed public health crisis, that enabled the creation of a strong, international pro sex work lobby group. Sex worker activists sometimes direct fury at those who point out the harms of prostitution, and this anger can influence feminists who have previously been critical of prostitution into changing their positions (B. Sullivan, 1994). In an example of this fury, Cheryl Overs refers to the work of academic feminists who challenge trafficking in women and are critical of prostitution as 'the drivel about sexual slavery that is produced in American "women's studies" departments and exported in a blatant act of cultural imperialism' (Doezema, 1998a, p. 206). The influence of the sex work position has been most marked in international health politics, UNAIDS and the ILO (Oriel, forthcoming). The position is a comfortable one for governments and UN agencies to adopt because it offers no challenge to the rights of men to buy women for sex. It represents a return to the 19th century situation before feminists initiated the campaign against the contagious diseases acts in the UK in the 1860s (Jeffreys, 1985a). At that time men's prostitution behaviour, that is buying women for sex, was an unchallenged prerogative. There were prostitution survivors who set up organizations in the 1980s and 1990s in the US from a very different viewpoint, such as WHIS-PER (Women Hurt in Systems of Prostitution Engaged in Revolt) (Giobbe, 1990) and SAGE (Standing Against Global Exploitation) (Hotaling, 1999) and Breaking Free (V. Carter, 1999). All these groups argue that prostitution should be understood as violence against women, but their views have not been so influential, perhaps because they do not fit the politics and practice of neo-liberal economics so well.

The sex work position appealed to socialist feminists in particular because they were prepared to see prostitution as an issue of workers' rights rather than one of violence against women. Socialist feminist theory and action have focused less on violence against women and more on issues of work and the economy. The sex work position had considerable influence on feminist debate, also, because many feminist academics and activists from different points of view were keen to listen to and respect the views of those women who represented themselves as having experience of prostitution, and spokespersons of sex work organizations were generally uncritical (Jeffreys, 1995). When some sex work groups said that prostitution was a positive experience, an exercise of personal choice and should be seen as legitimate work, some found it hard to disagree. The fact that there were survivors expressing very different perspectives, and that adoption of a sex work perspective involved a conscious choice to reject these other views, did not cause as much concern as it should have. Radical feminists, on the other hand, were not prepared to see prostitution as ordinary work because their backgrounds lay in researching and working on violence against women, particularly sexual violence. They recognized the similarities between the experience of prostituted women and rape victims, such as having to disassociate emotionally from their bodies to survive, and suffering symptoms of post-traumatic shock and negative feelings about their bodies and their selves (Jeffreys, 1997; Farley, 2003).

The radical feminist philosopher Kathy Miriam explains the apparently positive motivation behind the adoption of the pro sex work position. She says that this position 'casts sex workers' rights in terms of a politics of "recognition"' which 'pivots on "identity" as its moral/political fulcrum and aims at redressing injuries to status, for example stigma and degradation, as a basic harm or injustice inflicted on certain identity-groups' (Miriam, 2005, p. 7). When this approach is applied to prostitution, 'the stigmatization of prostitutes – rather than the structure of the practice itself – becomes the basic injustice to be redressed by pro-sex-work advocates' (ibid.). Miriam explains that though this approach may well be founded upon the positive motivation of dealing justice to a stigmatized group, it makes it very difficult to see the 'relations of dominance and subordination' that underlie prostitution, particularly in forms that go beyond obvious force. Though the impulse towards adopting a sex work position might have been progressive on the part of many of the theorists and activists who adopted it, the language and concepts of the position are precisely those that most suit the present economic ideology of neo-liberalism. They can, as Miriam points out, veer towards a decontextualized individualism of personal choice which is quite far from the politics of gender, race and class that is at the root of both socialist and radical feminism. They can even go so far as to support a free market, deregulationist approach to prostitution which suits the interests of sex industrialists rather than the girls and women caught up in the industry. Since radical feminists have focused more on the politics of the personal, such as how power relations are represented in women's everyday relationships with men, they have tended to be less well represented in theorizing international politics than socialist feminists. Those radical feminists who have been writing in the area of international politics have tended to concentrate on issues of violence against women, including prostitution (Kelly, 2000; Jeffreys, 1997; Barry, 1995). The sex work position has, therefore, tended to predominate in international feminist political theory through socialist feminist work which privileges a workers' rights or politics of identity approach.

Prostitution as reproductive labour

One upshot of the adoption of the sex work position is that many feminist theorists of the international political economy have lumped prostitution in with domestic labour in the category of 'reproductive labour' (Peterson, 2003; Jyoti Sanghera, 1997). When serious feminist critics of globalization mention prostitution it is usually not problematized, since reproductive labour is an area of women's work that such theorists tend to valorize in compensation for the way in which women's work, particularly unpaid work in the home, has been ignored in economic theory. Theorists such as Spike Peterson (2003), Barbara Ehrenreich and Arlie Hochschild

(2003), have pointed out that the 'service sector', which is becoming more and more significant in rich countries as manufacturing is outsourced to the poor world, represents to a large extent work that women have always carried out in the private sphere with no pay. Once commercialized as 'services', this work attracts payment in the form of domestic labour, or caring work. These writers, less convincingly, tack on prostitution to this analysis and point to 'sex work' being paid for as 'sexual services'. Identifying prostitution as a form of reproductive labour is a category error. Domestic labour fits this category in a way that prostitution does not, particularly because 'reproductive labour' is defined as 'socially necessary' (Peterson, 2003, p. 94; Jyoti Sanghera, 1997). Though arguably the preparation of food and care of children is 'socially necessary', and indeed men may, though they do not much at present, do it too, prostitution is not. The idea of 'social necessity' in relation to prostitution applies specifically to men. Prostitution is a socially constructed idea (Jeffreys, 1997) and behaviour which may be necessary to the maintenance of male dominance, but is not in any way socially necessary to women.

There is another problem with recognizing 'sexual services' as part of reproductive labour. This could imply that providing sexual access to men whilst they disassociate is an ordinary part of women's work in the home, which would undermine decades of feminist work to end the requirement that women engage in unwanted sex which has no connection with their pleasure. Prostitution may outsource that part of women's obligations under male domination that they most despise and are particularly harmed by. It is not the same as cleaning or baking cakes. One good indication of this is the fact that youth and inexperience are the most highly valued aspects of a girl inducted into prostitution. She will never be as valuable to her handlers as she is at the moment at which she is first raped, which may be as early as 10 years old (Saeed, 2001). Maids are not most valuable when they are children and do not know what they are doing. It is more useful to see prostitution as the outsourcing of women's subordination, rather than the outsourcing of an ordinary form of servicing work which just happens to be performed by women.

Choice and agency

The sex work position employs an individualist approach, representing the diverse aspects of prostitution, such as stripping, as areas in which women can exercise choice and agency or even be empowered (Hanna, 1998; Schweitzer, 1999; Liepe-Levinson, 2002; Egan, 2006). This approach is in rather sharp contradiction to the industrialization of prostitution which has been taking place in recent decades. As Carole Pateman points out, when socialist feminists adopt this approach to prostitution they end up being rather more positive and context blind in relation to prostitution than they would be towards other kinds of work, which are understood to be carried out in relations of domination and subordination (Pateman, 1988). Until recently the sex work position was mainly confined to research on forms of prostitution in the west, where prostituted women could be seen by 'choice' theorists as having the possibility of engaging in a variety of occupations to maintain subsistence. Now, however, the use of liberal individualist language, and even rational choice theory, has been extended to describe the most impressively unlikely situations in the non-west.

Alys Willman-Navarro, for instance, uses the language of rational choice in an issue of the journal *Research for Sex Work*, on 'Sex Work and Money' (2006). The journal publishes material from sex work organizations from different countries. She looks at research literature showing that prostituted women in Calcutta and Mexico engage in sex with prostitutors without condoms because they know 'sex workers who are willing to perform unprotected sex will be compensated for doing so, while those who prefer to use condoms earn less', a loss which can be as much as 79 per cent of earnings (Willman-Navarro, 2006, p. 18). Such research, she says, shows 'sex workers' as 'rational agents responding to incentives' (ibid., p. 19). The 'choice' between the chance of death from HIV/AIDS and the ability to feed and school her children does not offer sufficient realistic alternatives to qualify as an exercise in 'agency'. Nonetheless, Willman-Navarro remains upbeat in her approach: 'In Nicaragua I have met sex workers who are barely making ends meet. I have met others who send their children to some of the best schools in the capital ... They didn't do this by cashing in on one lucky night, but through years of rational choices.' Women in prostitution, this account tells us, can be successful entrepreneurs if only they act rationally.

Another example of this individualist approach can be found in the work of Travis Kong (2006) on prostituted women in Hong Kong. Kong's determination to respect the women as self-actualizing and possessed of agency leads to an individualist approach quite at odds with what the research itself reveals about the conditions of the women's existence. Kong takes the fashionable approach to prostitution of defining it as emotional labour. The concept of emotional labour, developed by Arlie Hochschild (1983), is very useful for analysing much of the paid and unpaid work that women do, such as that of cabin staff on aeroplanes. When this concept is carried over to prostitution, in which what is done to the inside and outside of women's bodies is the very heart of the 'work', it suggests a squeamishness about recognizing the physical details involved, and requires a mind/body split. A large part of the 'emotional' work of prostitution is the construction of measures to enable a disassociation of mind from body in order to survive the abuse (Farley, 2003). This is not a usual component of 'emotional labour'. Kong says that she will employ a 'poststructuralist conception of power and identity formation' and 'depict my respondents as performing the skilled emotional labour of sex in exchange for their clients' money ... I argue that their major problem is not with the commercial transaction ... but with the social stigma, surveillance and dangers at their workplaces' (Kong, 2006, p. 416). These women, Kong explains, are 'independent workers' and she expresses some disappointment at how 'apolitical and conventional' they are, in contrast with the 'image of a transgressive sexual and political minority that has been portrayed in the agency model of proprostitution feminism' (Kong, 2006, p. 415). But when the bald facts of their conditions of work are mentioned they seem to be about the use of their bodies rather than their minds: 'Since they have ejaculated on us ... They won't rape other women ... and they wouldn't lose their temper when they go home ... they won't ejaculate on their wives when they get home' (Kong, 2006, p. 420). The example given of how they have to develop 'skilled work techniques' is 'they have to learn to do fellatio' (Kong, 2006, p. 423). It is interesting to note that a 2007 report on the Australian sex industry states, for the benefit of those seeking to set up brothels, that the work requires no skills training (IBISWorld, 2007).

The postcolonial approach

Exponents of the sex work position can be very critical of those feminists who seek to abolish prostitution and the traffic in women. One major form of criticism is that feminists who seek to abolish prostitution 'victimize' prostituted women by not recognizing their 'agency'.

This has been employed against anti-trafficking campaigners and feminists who seek to end prostitution, who are said to 'victimize' prostituted women (Kapur, 2002). This criticism is not newly minted in relation to prostitution, but has been common to liberal feminist criticisms of the anti-rape and anti-pornography movements such as the work of Katie Roiphe in the US (Roiphe, 1993; Denfeld, 1995). US liberal feminists of the early 1990s argued that it is important to recognize women's sexual agency. They said that harping on about sexual violence and the harms that women suffer at the hands of men showed a lack of respect for women's sexual choices and sexual freedom. It is interesting to note that this idea has been taken up by postcolonial feminists to criticize radical feminists, as in the work of Ratna Kapur (2002).

Kapur says that those who 'articulate' the 'victim subject', such as suggesting that prostituted women are oppressed or harmed, base their arguments on 'gender essentialism' and generalizations which reflect the problems of privileged white, western, middle-class, heterosexual women (Kapur, 2002, p. 6). This accusation implies that those who identify women as being oppressed are 'classist' through the very fact of making that identification. Such arguments are based on 'cultural essentialism' too, portraying women as victims of their culture, Kapur says. Those guilty of these racist and classist practices are those involved in working against violence. She identifies Catharine MacKinnon and Kathleen Barry in particular, and anti-trafficking campaigners who 'focus on violence and victimization'. Campaigns against violence against women, she says, 'have taken feminists back into a protectionist and conservative discourse' (ibid., p. 7). Anti-violence feminists are accused of using 'metanarratives' and erasing the differences between women, and of a lack of complexity that 'sets up a subject who is thoroughly disempowered and helpless' (ibid., p. 10). However, it is not just 'western' feminists that Kapur criticizes for these solecisms, but Indian ones too who happen to be anti-violence campaigners. They too negate the 'very possibility of choice or agency' by saying that 'sex work' in South Asia is a form of exploitation (ibid., p. 26). She is critical of what she perceives as an alliance between 'Western feminists and Indian feminists' in the human rights arena as a result of which '[t]he victim subject has become a de-contextualised, ahistorical subject, disguised superficially as the dowry victim, as the victim of honour killings, or as the victim of trafficking and prostitution' (ibid., p. 29).

Another argument that Kapur makes is that prostitution is transgressive. This idea fits into the pro sexual freedom position of the new left which led to the promotion of pornography by those creating the 1960s and 1970s 'counterculture' (see Jeffreys, 1990/91). She argues that the correct approach for feminist theorists is, therefore, to 'focus on moments of resistance' and thus disrupt the 'linear narrative produced by the VAW [violence against women] campaigns' and this will 'complicate the binary of the West and the Rest' (ibid., p. 29). She explains that she chooses to do this by foregrounding the 'sex worker' because '[h]er claims as a parent, entertainer, worker and sexual subject disrupt dominant sexual and familial norms. In post-colonial India, her repeated performances also challenge and alter dominant cultural norms. From her peripheral location, the sex worker brings about a normative challenge by negotiating her disclaimed or marginalized identity within more stable and dominant discourses' (ibid., p. 31). But the idea that prostituted women transgress the social norms of heterosexuality and the heteropatriarchal family is by no means clear in India and Pakistan, where forms of family prostitution thrive (Saeed, 2001; Agrawal, 2006b).

In her research on family prostitution in Bombay in the 1920s and 1930s, Ashwini Tambe specifically refutes the notion that prostituted women should be seen as transgressive (Tambe, 2006). She stresses the continuities between families and brothels. She says that feminist theory is wrong in always locating prostitution 'outside the ambit of official familial institutions' (Tambe, 2006, p. 220). She criticizes the idea put forward by what she calls 'sex radicals' that prostitution has the potential to 'sever the link between sex and long-term intimacy and allow the performance of undomesticated sexualities that challenge common prescriptions of feminine passivity' (ibid., p. 221). What, she asks, 'do we make of sex workers who are, effectively, domesticated?' (ibid., p. 221). She cites national studies from India in the present that show that for 32 per cent of prostituted women 'kith and kin' were responsible for their entry into prostitution, and that 82 per cent of prostituted women in Bombay have and raise children in brothels. Precisely similar family structures exist in Calcutta's brothels too, she points out. Many prostituted women remain in brothels because they have been born there. In her historical study she found that husbands and mothers delivered girls and women to brothels. Brothel keepers adopted maternal roles towards the girls delivered to them. Family members put girls into prostitution through the devadasi system, and in castes that traditionally practised 'entertainment' for their livelihood, girls and women supported whole families through prostitution combined with dancing and music. Tambe 'cautions against' the celebration of the 'liberatory potential of sex work and brothel life' and is critical of 'sex radicals' who say that 'sex work can be a source of agency and resistance' (ibid., p. 236–7).

But Kapur goes further in her romanticization of prostitution, stating that the agency of the women that the anti-violence perspective turns into 'victims' is 'located in the recognition that the post-colonial subject can and does dance, across the shaky edifice of gender and culture, bringing to this project the possibility of imagining a more transformative and inclusive politics' (Kapur, 2002, p. 37). In her laudatory commentary on Kapur's work, Jane Scoular makes the basis of this approach, which she identifies as 'postmodern', plain. She says such theorizing, 'by maintaining a critical distance from oppressive structural factors', enables theorists 'to resist attempts to see power as overwhelming and consuming the subject', thus creating space for a 'transformative' feminist theory which seeks to 'utilize the disruptive potential of the counter-hegemonic and "resisting" subject to challenge hierarchical relations' (Scoular, 2004, p. 352). If power relations are downplayed, then it is easier to see prostituted women as 'dancing'. In contrast, *The Industrial Vagina* is diametrically opposed to the idea of keeping a distance from 'structural factors' that underlie prostitution; rather, I seek to make them more visible.

Kapur's approach is echoed in the work of Jo Doezema, who argues that 'western' feminists victimize Third World prostituted women (Doezema, 2001). She too is savagely critical of the work of feminist anti-trafficking campaigners such as Kathleen Barry and the Coalition Against Trafficking in Women (CATW), accusing them of what she calls 'neo-colonialism' in their attitude to Third World prostituted women (ibid.). She says that the attitude 'that Third World women – and prostitutes in particular – are victims of their (backward, barbaric) cultures is pervasive in the rhetoric of CATW' (Doezema, 2001, p. 30). She is harsh in her criticism of feminists engaged in anti-trafficking work, saying that they are engaged in 'relations of domination and subordination' (ibid., p. 23), i.e. the feminists are the oppressors here, a construction which very effectively disappears male domination from the picture. But, like Kapur, she has to deal with the problem that, as she admits, many activist Indian feminists are also abolitionists and involved in CATW. In her account these women become 'dupes' for accepting a western, colonialist position on prostitution and abandoning their own best interests.

Though Doezema is relentlessly positive in relation to prostitution in her more recent writings and advocacy work, it is interesting to note that she was rather candid about the harms of prostitution as she herself experienced them in Amsterdam, before she became involved in the Network of Sex Workers' Projects. In an interview from the mid-1990s she said 'all brothels are actually shit' (Chapkis, 1997, p. 117). She said, 'you are kind of struggling the whole time to keep the client from doing things you don't want and trying to keep him satisfied at the same time' (ibid., p. 119). On one occasion in escort work she had a 'client' who was 'really really drunk and a little bit crazy and … I don't think about it a lot actually' (ibid., p. 119). She was in such danger that she says she did not tell her friends because '[t]hey would have said, "You are stopping; don't ever do this again." I didn't want to stop, so I never dared tell anybody' (ibid., p. 120). She comments that 'for almost everybody I make it more positive than it is, because everybody has such a negative idea about it already. So you tend to only talk about the good things or the funny things' (ibid., p. 120). In other words she deliberately downplays the severe harms of prostitution that she has experienced. Her attitude towards having to suffer unwanted sex acts, which would be called sexual harassment or sexual assault outside the prostitution context, is to blame herself: 'Sure, there are still times when I put up with something from a client that I don't want to have happen, either because I'm too tired, or I don't know how to say that I don't want it. But I have learned now to deal with that; instead of thinking, "Oh, I'm the worst whore in the world", I just think, "Okay, next time better"' (ibid., p. 122). Currently Doezema, along with other sex worker activist colleagues, minimizes the harms of prostitution in order to achieve the decriminalization of the industry. The minimization of harm is a common practice amongst prostituted women, who routinely block out or downplay the violence they experience both inside and outside prostitution (Kelly and Radford, 1990; Gorkoff and Runner, 2003).

Radical feminist responses to the 'agency' approach

The pro sex work approach to the industry of prostitution has been strongly challenged on many levels by radical feminist critics. Radical feminist theorists have been sharply critical in particular of what they identify as the liberal individualism of scholars and activists who emphasize the importance of women's 'agency' and concentrate on the freedom of action of the individual prostituted woman in contradiction to the oppressive relations of power within which she acts (Pateman, 1988; Miriam, 2005). The 'agency' approach is used in feminist theory in relation to other issues such as the veil, makeup and fashion, as well as sexual practice. Rosalind Gill has addressed the problems involved in this approach to the politics of appearance (Gill, 2007). She explains that an approach which focuses on 'autonomous choices' 'remains complicit with, rather than critical of, postfeminist and neoliberal discourses that see individuals as entrepreneurial actors who are rational, calculating and self-regulating' (Gill, 2007, p. 74). Pro sex work writers practise precisely the problematic approach she criticizes in their interpretation of the experiences of trafficked women: 'The neoliberal subject is required to bear full responsibility for their life biography no matter how severe the constraints upon their action ... Just as neoliberalism requires individuals to narrate their life story as if it were the outcome of deliberative choices' (ibid.). She asks why it is that so much feminist theory has taken up choice language and suggests that it is because a postfeminist perspective no longer allows recognition of the oppression of women: 'Is there a subtext to this? A postfeminist subtext that no longer views women as oppressed' (ibid.).

Kathy Miriam addresses the way the 'agency' approach is employed in relation to trafficking in women in particular and characterizes well the problematic liberal individualism that underlies this approach (Miriam, 2005). She argues that the sex work approach 'depends on a contractual, liberal model of agency that both conceals and presupposes the demand side of the institution of prostitution' and also conceals the power relations within which women are prostituted (Miriam, 2005, p. 2). The radical feminist approach, on the other hand, 'radically *challenges* feminism to theorize power and agency *outside a liberal framework*' (ibid., p. 2). The power relations in which prostitution takes place are founded, she argues, using Pateman's excellent development of this concept (Pateman, 1988), on the male sex right. Under male domination, she explains, 'men's right to be sexually serviced is non-negotiable whatever else women can negotiate' (ibid., p. 14).

It is the fact that the male sex right cannot be questioned that creates the greatest challenge for feminists in the anti-prostitution struggle: 'this legitimized and entrenched relation defined by men's right to demand access to women is the central conception of male power at stake for the feminist movement to abolish prostitution' (ibid., p. 13). Under a political system in which this male demand is understood as simply ordinary sex drive, or sexual initiation, the whole idea of women being able to express 'sexual agency', an idea central to the pro sex work position, becomes problematic. They may only express 'agency' through answering the demand and allowing access; no other possibility is open. But because the male sex drive is seen as a fact of life, the very demand for prostitution itself is unquestioned. The pro sex work lobby cannot see this because 'male power is invisible to it as *domination* and only intelligible as *coercive force*' (ibid.). Miriam makes the important point that agency and oppression are not in contradiction to one another. Women exercise agency in order to survive the power relations and oppressive circumstances in which they find themselves. The theoretical task, Miriam argues, is for radical feminist theory to 'theorize freedom in terms of women's collective political agency (power to): this task requires an understanding that freedom is not negotiating within a situation taken as inevitable, but rather, a capacity to radically transform and/or determine the situation itself' (ibid., p. 14). The very general acceptance within feminist activism and theory of the sex work position represents an accommodation to the male dominant construction of men's sexual drive and men's right to commandeer the bodies of women in which to act it out. In that sense it is a defeat of the idea that feminism can recreate sex as eroticized equality (Jeffreys, 1990/91), and release women from the tyranny of the male sex right.

The earnings of prostituted women

Though women may, in the sex work approach, be seen as exercising 'agency' this is unlikely to bring them great economic benefit, though they may earn more than other unskilled women. The approach which emphasizes the rational choice of women to enter prostitution on the grounds of the fine earnings they can make therein (Willman-Navarro, 2006) is contradicted by some more critical and carefully calculated analysis. Research is just beginning to take place into the economics of prostitution from the point of view of the women who are prostituted. Though prostitution forms an increasingly profitable global economic sector, the profits are largely going to those who control the business rather than to the individual prostituted women themselves. Prostituted women in Hong Kong, for instance, barely make enough to survive. The NGO Zi Teng (2006), writing about Chinese migrant 'sex workers' in Hong Kong, explains that there is a redundant labour force of 150 million people in the Chinese countryside. The higher unemployment rates among women cause them to move to Hong Kong and into prostitution, where they earn meagre wages of $20 per 'service' and have an average of three customers per day. Zi Teng describes the physical abuse they suffer and the problem of being robbed. As is common in prostitution, they engage in sex without condoms in order to get the few customers they are able to attract. The majority of the prostituted women Zi Teng studied would 'not absolutely insist their customers use condoms'. Zi Teng does not place this in such a positive light as Willman-Navarro (2006), however, and explains the lack of condom use as the result of customer reluctance and the concern of the prostituted women not to 'affect the business' (Zi Teng, 2006, p. 30).

The situation was not markedly different for prostituted women in New York. Juhu Thukral, in a study of 'Sex Workers and Finances' in New York City, found that prostitution was not regular work for the 52 women she interviewed (Thukral, 2006, p. 22). The women 'moved in and out of indoor sex work' and 'the money made through sex work is often quickly made and quickly spent', which kept the women in prostitution. Half of the women wanted to save money but found that very hard. Thirty-eight per cent of participants said that they 'did not regularly meet their financial goal when working ... The four trafficked women reported being physically and verbally abused when they fell short' (ibid., p. 23). The situation of trafficked women was particularly dire: 'Trafficked women were rarely able to keep the money they earned, which was reported as low as $13 per client, or just over half the takings of a $25 session in a brothel catering to Latino immigrants' (ibid., p. 23). The need to make some money vied with the desire to keep themselves safe, so one respondent described how she would only 'go out with clients' when 'high'. If sober she preferred to go hungry rather than face the dangers. Prostituted women in New York City might be expected to gain more economic benefit from prostitution than women in poor countries, but this is clearly not necessarily the case. A 2006 report on the legalized brothel and strip club industry in Australia, while waxing lyrical about the increased profitability of the industry, quotes a Sydney survey which found that, after brothel charges, one-third of women earned up to $500 each week, about 20 per cent earned $800–$1,000 and another 20 per cent earned more than $1,000 (IBISWorld, 2007). These are certainly not high earnings, and are likely to be restricted to the short number of years that the women remain in the industry. They do not reveal what the women are able to earn on leaving. Nonetheless the report states that average wages had decreased in the previous five years as a result of greater competition. The success of the industry, it seems, may disadvantage prostituted women.

One particularly impressive study does look at the effect of prostitution on a woman's economic prospects over the life cycle. Linda DeRiviere examined, through eight case studies and 54 interviews, the economics of prostitution in the life experience of prostituted women in Canada. Most of the women were aboriginal and had worked in a variety of prostitution settings (DeRiviere, 2006). She explains that '[c]urrent literature in North America is riddled with debate about whether prostitution is a profit-making and empowering venture of rational, utility-maximising actors' (ibid., p. 367). 'Most', she says, 'propose that prostitution is financially lucrative' and equate 'the sex trade with entrepreneurial skills'. They represent the 'choice' to enter 'sex work' as a rational decision in which the individual 'weighs personal costs and benefits or the expected utility of engaging in this lifestyle'. DeRiviere, in contrast, looks at prostitution in Winnipeg, Canada, over the life cycle. It usually begins in adolescent years, with Canadian research showing that 96 per cent of women enter prostitution before 17 years, and thus leads to 'opportunity costs' such as the loss of education, skills, work experience and on-the-job training which could enable prostituted women to leave prostitution and move on to another occupation. It is a temporary situation for most but has a permanent effect on lifetime earnings and productive outcomes. Her research subjects were overwhelmingly (90.3 per cent) indigenous women. In Canada, as she explains, indigenous women are hugely overrepresented in prostitution (see also Gorkoff and Runner, 2003; Farley and Lynne, 2004). The gross earnings of her respondents were $27,071 but the women did not receive this amount for their own use as 'transfers to pimps and dependent partners and escort agency owners' amounted to $10,068 annually, or 37.2 per cent. Drugs and alcohol, which are necessary to enable the women to survive prostitution and disassociate from the abuse, accounted for $12,617, or 46.6 per cent. Lost earnings following violent incidents etc. amounted to $2,305, or 8.5 per cent. Thus the net annual surplus funds after subtracting substantial costs are less than 8 per cent of gross earnings.

The women she studied suffered reduced lifelong earnings as a result of the physical and mental health issues which resulted from prostitution, the costs of which, in DeRiviere's estimation, far exceeded the benefits over the woman's lifetime. She concludes, from her eight case studies, 'that throughout the period of involvement in the sex trade, a small earnings premium is the only direct benefit of prostitution at a personal level. However, such benefits are short term relative to the individual's available working years, and the offsetting costs of prostitution are huge' (DeRiviere, 2006, p. 379).

The development of prostitution

Despite the negative effects of prostitution on the lives of individual women, there has been a tendency in feminist theory to be upbeat and positive towards the contribution prostituted women make to 'development'. Feminist theorizing of prostitution has not paid much critical attention to the role of prostitution in development, and the variety of ways in which prostitution is linked with development are not yet included in development studies. If writers mention prostitution at all it is likely to be in the context of how useful the remittances of prostituted women are to the development of the economies of their countries of origin. Those who take a sex work approach see the prostitution of women who 'migrate for labour', meaning those who have been trafficked into debt bondage since women from poor countries do not have the resources or knowhow to 'migrate' under their own steam, as being positively beneficial for developing countries. Though prostitution does not bring about large profits for the vast majority of prostituted women, women are good at repatriating to their home countries as much of their earnings as they are able to spare from their own subsistence. This is in contrast to the behaviour of male migrants, who are likely to spend much more of what they earn, including expenditure for their own behaviour as prostitutors of their own countrywomen or others in their worksites (Pesar and Mahler, 2003). Laura Agustin, for instance, argues that prostitution is economically valuable in a piece entitled 'Contributing to "Development": Money Made Selling Sex'. It is valuable, she says, because, 'recent studies reveal how money sent home by migrants finances important social and structural projects known as "development" ... This goes for money made picking strawberries ... and selling sex ... the amounts mean the same no matter how they were earned, and they are used to finance construction projects, small businesses and cooperative agriculture for families, communities and whole regions' (Agustin, 2006b, p. 10). She says that 'most cultures do have their own visions of developing, and migrants who send money home contributed to the realisation of those visions, including the millions who sell sex' (ibid., p. 10).

Jyoti Sanghera makes the same argument. She says prostituted women contribute to the development of their 'larger cultural communities by financing the construction of schools, religious shrines, post offices and other public service facilities. Remittances of their earnings from abroad help their governments service the national debt of the country' (Sanghera, 1997, p. 10). Moreover, Sanghera argues, encouraging governments to assess the value of prostitution to their economies would be helpful: 'Societies that allow sex businesses to flourish and proliferate could include them in government accounting' (ibid.). This positive approach does not factor in the harms of prostitution to the life-courses and economic possibilities of those who are prostituted. It does not consider the expenses that states may have to enter into in order to support the girls and women who have been harmed when through age or physical and mental health problems they are no longer valuable to the industry, the expenses of policing and the operation of the legal system involved in combating trafficking and other problems integral to the industry.

There is no question that the prostitution of women has played a significant role in the development of many national economies and continues to do so. What is in question is whether this should be celebrated or condemned. The role of black slavery in the construction of British economic supremacy in the 19th century, for instance, is considered a cause for shame rather than celebration (Fryer, 1989). It is not obvious that the contribution of prostituted women in debt bondage should receive a much more positive treatment. There is evidence of the way in which the prostitution of girls and women has contributed to the historical economic development of Japan and Australia. The foundation of the 'comfort women' system for the Japanese military in the 1930s and 1940s lies in the phenomenon of karayuki-san in the second half of the 19th century (Tanaka, 2002). Young women and girls from poor rural areas were kidnapped, deceived by being offered jobs or sold by their parents to traffickers, through very similar methods to those used today in the trafficking in women. They were smuggled out of Japan and sold to brothels in neighbouring countries, in particular China and the east coast of Russia. The children, some of whom were as young as seven when sold, were raised and trained in brothels in the major business centres for this industry, Vladivostok, Shanghai and Singapore. They were trafficked on to brothels in South East Asia, India, Australia, Hawaii, the East Coast of the US, and even Cape Town. In the decades after 1868 their numbers increased rapidly. The trafficking of karayuki replicates closely the trafficking that takes place today. The girls were sold for $500–800 to brothels and were then in debt bondage, often finding themselves tied into servicing the debt for many years. Many never saw their homes again, and many committed suicide. By 1910 the number of registered karayuki-san was more than 19,000, whereas their equivalent in prostitution within Japan numbered only 47,541. The trafficking was well organized through established crime organizations such as the Yakuza which were traditionally involved in this trade.

Yuki Tanaka uses the work of Japanese feminist historians from as early as the 1950s to argue that this form of trafficking in women was crucial to the rapid economic and industrial development of Japan in this period. But this importance was long neglected in scholarship. This neglect was perhaps similar to the neglect until comparatively recently of acknowledgement of the role of black slavery in the development of British capitalism (Fryer, 1989). Japan's domestic licensed prostitution system, on which high tax rates were levied, also played an important part in 'raising public money when the government needed large sums to build the basic economic infrastructure' (Tanaka, 2002, p. 182). The overseas prostitution business, however, was an important source for the acquisition of much needed foreign currency. There is evidence for its significance in the fact that out of a total of 1,000,000 yen that Japanese residents in Vladivostok remitted home to Japan in 1900, 630,000 yen was from earnings in prostitution. In the trafficking hub of Singapore most Japanese residents were dependent on servicing the industry of prostitution, including retail dealers, drapers, photographers, doctors and brothel keepers. Japanese trade followed the karayuki-san, rather than the other way about. As Tanaka comments: 'It can be said that Japan's modern international trade developed from such small-scale retail trade beginnings which followed the expansion of the traffic in Japanese women in the Asia-Pacific region' (Tanaka, 2002, p. 170).

Even after World War II, Tanaka points out, the prostitution of local women was used in economic reconstruction as they were placed into a new 'comfort system', this time to acquire dollars from GIs. He comments that Japan's sex industry was so closely intertwined with the development of Japanese capitalism that it may be 'unusual to find another nation that exploited women for sex to that extent' (ibid., p. 182). As Susan Brownmiller tellingly remarks in her preface to Tanaka's book: 'The moral lawlessness accompanying crude, rudimentary capitalism is not very different from the brutal sexual exploitation that accompanies warfare' (Brownmiller, 1975, p. xvi). This moral lawlessness has continued to create prostitution industries in countries engaged in the rogue capitalism of the free market today. Other poor Asian countries followed Japan's example a century later when the Philippines and Thailand made the sale of women's bodies vital to their economies.

Raelene Frances' work on the history of prostitution in Australia gives useful information about how the trafficked Japanese girls were used there (Frances, 2007). They were taken in debt bondage to outback mining towns like Kalgoorlie in West Australia for the sexual use of the isolated male workforces of those areas in the late 19th century, and can thus be seen as having played an important part in enabling Australia's economic development. Australia's present-day wealth owes something to the prostitution of these women in conditions of servitude. The prostitution of convict women, some of whom were already prostituted before transportation or prostituted aboard the ships to Australia, and many of whom had no other chance of survival on arrival, was also necessary to the foundation of Australia as a functional economy. Frances explains that the prostitution of convict women was undertaken by those entrusted with their care, who set up brothels in the warehouse accommodation they were put into when they got off the ships (ibid.). This is not the only form of slavery employed in Australia's economic development since there was enslavement of aboriginal people and the trafficking of Torres Strait Islander people into a variety of forms of labour as well. But the contribution of prostituted women in debt bondage to Australia's prosperity, particularly its mining industry, has not been so much remarked. Frances has also researched the ways in which aboriginal women were kidnapped or leased through the exchange of gifts from the men with rights over them. They were used sexually as well as for domestic and other forms of labour in remote areas of western and northern Australia, on farming and cattle properties, by pearldivers in Broome, by fisherman and traders from Indonesia on the northern coasts (Frances, 2007). Unfortunately economic development in many countries and in many forms is increasingly dependent on the prostitution of women today, and this needs to be a concern of feminist globalization literature.

Feminist literature in development studies has begun to address the problem of violence against women, but not yet prostitution (Sweetman, 1998a). Non-governmental organizations (NGOs) involved in development are increasingly concerned to alleviate the violence which already exists in patriarchal cultures within which they operate, but the fact that violence against women can be a result of the development process is only just beginning to be recognized. Caroline Sweetman comments that 'there is evidence that violence against women increases in intensity where gender relations are being transformed and male privilege is challenged' (Sweetman, 1998b, p. 5). She calls upon development organizations to recognize 'the existence of violence against women as a barrier to development' (ibid., p. 6). Thus in Papua New Guinea NGO efforts to give women more opportunities of education are hampered by the fact that the dominant status of male partners might be undermined and result in greater battering of women seeking to attend classes. As economic development takes place, traditional structures of male dominance are undermined in other ways too. Village life, in which girls and women gained some protection through the males who had rights over them, and through traditional cultural restraints, is being replaced by urban growth, the creation of truck routes and mining camps, and girls and women are moving about more freely as well as taking part in economic activities. All of this has contributed to a wave of very severe violence against girls and women, including a high rate of gang rape (Jenkins, 2006). The development of violence against women is taking place in relation to economic change in many countries in Latin America, such as border towns in Mexico and in Guatemala (Amnesty International, 2006c), resulting in the killing of women and girls in their hundreds yearly. In Cambodia the practice of gang rape has developed considerably in response to women's increasing mobility and economic participation (Jejeebhoy *et al.*, 2005), such that 61 per cent of male university students admit to having engaged in this activity against prostituted girls, 'beer' girls and other young women in the workforce who can be seen as departing from traditional roles and being fair game. Violence against women is a most important area for development studies that is beginning to receive attention, but the way in which prostitution is linked to development is much less understood.

Prostitution is created, even in cultures which have not known any form of the practice previously, to service male workers in economic development projects such as mining and logging camps, where it negatively affects the health and opportunities of women and girls at very young ages, and undermines the traditional ways in which women and men relate (Wardlow, 2007). Cynthia Enloe, whose work is always breaking new ground in forcing attention to the harms suffered by women in international economic and military development, pointed out the problem of the prostitution of girls and women on banana plantations in Brazil, for instance (Enloe, 1989). Mining and logging camps create the same harms to girls. Children are being prostituted in the Solomon Islands logging industry (*Taranaki Daily News*, 2007). A Church of Melanesia study found that 'Malaysian loggers in the Solomon Islands are involved in horrific sexual abuse of village children who are being raped, sold into marriage and used for pornography' (ibid.). In one small area 73 children had been 'exploited'. The logging industry is dominated by Malaysians but the clear-felled timber is shipped to China for projects such as building the Beijing Olympic facilities. An islander who had worked in a logging camp explained: 'There were seven Malaysian men there, and every one was married to a young girl, aged 13 or 14. They are not interested in the older girls – once they are 18. I don't know what the arrangement was – if they got money. But they must' (ibid.). A nine-year-old girl who was interviewed said that her father had taken her to the camp, where 'I have seen Malaysian men touching their house girls' breasts. They used to do that to their house girls. While they were eating, they would have one hand on their spoon (eating), and one hand on a girl's breast'. Children are sold into temporary 'marriages' in the camps by their parents. Bride price is a harmful cultural practice in the Solomons so this new form of prostitution is simply a development of this patriarchal tradition. In the port of Honiara itself girls as young as 12 are reportedly working as 'dugongs', which is the local name for prostituted children. They service foreign freighters that anchor to collect tuna caught by local fishing boats (Callinan, 2006). A 2004 UNICEF study found dozens of examples of sexual abuse of children, 'from underage prostitution to the manufacture of child pornography, child sex tourism and marriages of convenience'. Nine boys aged 6–14 survived on the streets by having sex with the crews of Japanese fishing boats. One commented: 'It is very painful but I need money for food' (ibid.).

Shamima Ali's research for UNICEF in 2006 on violence against the girl child in 14 Pacific Island states demonstrates the ways in which economic development is creating severe problems of sexual violence against girls and women, including prostitution (Ali, 2006). She documents the same custom of parents selling girl children to logging and mining workers in Papua New Guinea, under the guise of original customs such as bride price which 'have been modified to suit the needs of the males in the family' (ibid., p. 6). Even the introduction of education can have harmful effects on girls, as some teachers ask for sex from students to pay the school fee (ibid.). Carol Jenkins' work on the changing sexual culture in Papua New Guinea as a result of economic development and the importation of pornography explains that from the 1930s onwards Australian administrators, miners and policemen exchanged trade goods for access to local women as they opened up the Highlands for profit (Jenkins, 2006, p. 27). Mining was cited, however, as a contributor to the growth of prostitution as early as 1900. From the earliest days when the colonizers began to develop mining, a prostitution industry was created, in a culture in which it had not existed, for male workers recruited locally. By 1970, when prostitution was being documented in urban and rural areas, it was contributing to the spread of syphilis. The negative consequences of economic development in the prostitution of women and girls need to be taken seriously. The ethical concerns that are considered in relation to mining and logging developments need to include the construction of prostitution alongside issues of land rights, human rights and environmental destruction. The harms of prostitution can perhaps become visible if the bodies of girls are seen as part of the environment too. Discussion of human rights and gender equality in development in relation to mining now includes consideration of violence against women and HIV but not yet prostitution (Macdonald, 2003). The creation of prostitution is a serious obstacle to the stated aim of the International Labour Organization of creating 'fair globalization'.

Conclusion

When feminist theorizing of prostitution frames the practice as ordinary work which enables women to express 'choice' and 'agency', and represents trafficked women in debt bondage as simply 'migrating for labour', it serves to normalize the industry and support its growth. It airbrushes the harms that girls and women suffer in prostitution and makes it very difficult for feminist activists to oppose the construction of prostitution industries as an ordinary part of economic development, and demand dignified work for women. Such theorizing also supports the campaign by the prostitution industry, sex work organizations and some governments to legalize or decriminalize prostitution. For the industry to prosper, toleration is good, but legalization is better. Thus the approaches that feminist theorists choose to take have important implications. The growth of the industry multiplies the harms that are an integral part of prostitution and other forms of sexual exploitation whether 'legal' or not. The sex industry cannot be quarantined, set apart from the rest of the society for men to abuse the women caught within the industry in seclusion. Approaches to prostitution which focus on 'choice' and 'agency' are profoundly unsuitable to address the conditions in which the vast majority of women and girls enter and struggle to survive in prostitution, as the following chapters will demonstrate.

Chapter 2

Marriage and prostitution

In 2007 the UN Trafficking Rapporteur identified trafficking in women for marriage, in such practices as the mail order bride industry and forced marriage, as a significant aspect of the trafficking in women which needed to be addressed (UNHRC, 2007a). This is an important extension of feminist and human rights analysis of trafficking in women. It places the spotlight on marriage, which has not usually been associated with prostitution in contemporary human rights scholarship. As the Rapporteur's report points out, marriage is often a straightforwardly economic transaction, in which sexual access to girls and women is purchased through bride price or a fee to an introduction agency. An understanding of the dynamics of marriage is helpful as a basis for an examination of the global industry of prostitution because it illustrates that prostitution is not just a form of ordinary ungendered work, like domestic labour or tomato picking, but has its origin, and its counterpart, in traditional forms of exchange of girls and women for cash or goods, in a form of chattel slavery (Rubin, 1975). Not all forms of marriage include the element of giving cash or goods in exchange for the woman or girl, but forms which do, such as child marriage, temporary marriage, the trafficking of women for marriage in India and China, and even concubinage, are increasing in many countries. The mail order bride industry has integrated the sale of women for sexual and other purposes into the global sex industry and the global economy. Where marriage is the result of sale or any form of commercial exchange it can be hard to distinguish this particular harmful practice from prostitution. I refer to this practice as servile marriage. Where no direct financial exchange takes place, but women are trapped by poverty and lack of remedy such as divorce, marriage still contains the aspect of prostitution since women have to allow sexual access to their bodies in return for subsistence.

The United Nations convention on marriage of 1964 shows a clear awareness of the harms to the human rights of women and girls involved in traditional practices that create servile marriages. The convention requires 'full and free consent' for marriage, that states specify a minimum age of marriage, though not what that age should be, and that marriages should be registered (United Nations, 1964). It 'reaffirms' in the preamble that all states 'should take all appropriate measures with a view to abolishing such customs, ancient laws and practices by ensuring, *inter alia*, complete freedom in the choice of a spouse, eliminating completely child marriages and the betrothal of young girls before the age of puberty, establishing appropriate penalties where necessary and establishing a civil or other register in which all marriages will be recorded'. The confidence of the marriage convention that servile marriage could be brought to an end looks strangely out of place today. Many of the practices have become sources of concern in western nations as they are practised by some members of immigrant or indigenous communities. Even at the time that the convention was promulgated critics attacked it on the grounds of cultural relativism and it had to be defended by such arguments as the fact that many non-western nations supported the convention (Schwelb, 1963). In more recent decades some feminist scholars have developed defences of practices such as arranged marriage and early marriage from a cultural relativist perspective, which have undermined human rights approaches to the problems (Moschetti, 2006).

Surprisingly, marriage and prostitution are often seen as polar opposites and distinguished from one another. The operation of this distinction is particularly clear in the phenomenon of 'temporary marriages', called mut'a or sigheh amongst Shi'ite muslims, where 'marriage' even for a couple of hours, for sexual purposes with payment to the woman, is seen as religiously acceptable whilst prostitution is totally condemned (Haeri, 1992). To eyes untrained in such religious distinctions it can be hard to see the difference. Feminist theorists, indeed, for more than two centuries have argued that prostitution and marriage are but two aspects of the one problem (Jeffreys, 1985b; Pateman, 1988). The problem is that, under male dominance, women are forced to submit their bodies to men's use in exchange for subsistence, or even, in the case of the honour killings of girls who reject arranged marriages, to escape assassination. This exchange of women between men has been recognized in the work of Lévi-Strauss as the very basis of the organization of society and culture. Gayle Rubin criticized the fact that Lévi-Strauss seemed to accept this exchange as just the way things were without recognizing the oppression of women involved (Rubin, 1975). She says that the usefulness of his concept was that 'it suggests that we look for the ultimate locus of women's oppression within the traffic in women, rather than within the traffic in merchandise' (ibid., p. 175). The exchange of women was specifically between men since men were the gift givers and women the gifts. The system was for the benefit of men because '[t]he relations of such a system are such that women are no longer in a position to realize the benefits of their own circulation … it is men who are the beneficiaries of the product of such exchanges – social organization' (ibid., p. 174).

In this chapter I will look at the ways in which feminists have made the connections between marriage and prostitution. I will examine the development of the forms of marriage which are most difficult to distinguish from prostitution, such as the mail order bride industry, into profitable market sectors and argue that forms of servile marriage do, like prostitution, commercialize the subordination of women.

Marriage and prostitution in feminist theory

In every outbreak of feminist activity from the late 18th century onwards, the similarities between marriage and prostitution have been theorized and often made central to analysis. Thus as early as 1790 Mary Wollstonecraft called marriage 'legal prostitution' (quoted in Pateman, 1988, p.190). Mrs Lucinda B. Chandler, speaking on the need to reform marriage at an international women's conference in the US in 1888, expostulated: 'Women as well as men must eliminate from marriage the features of prostitution, for when prostitution ceases inside of marriage it will disappear outside' (quoted in Jeffreys, 1985a, p. 23). British feminist activists against prostitution were often quite explicit about the similarities between these institutions of male dominance. Thus Elizabeth Wolstenholme Elmy, who combined the surname of her partner with her own, and would not have married him but for pressure from other feminists in the 1880s to be respectable, saw the 'bodily slavery' of women as forming the foundation of both systems (Jeffreys, 1985a, p. 34). 'Free love' feminists who rejected marriage altogether in the 1890s and sought a different way to conduct relationships with men in which they would not have to relinquish control over their own bodies and souls, spoke of marriage having evolved into 'that terrible growth, prostitution' (ibid., p. 43). In the decade before World War I the feminist playwright Cicely Hamilton saw marriage as a trade with insupportable conditions of work. These included lack of payment, sexual subjection and occupational hazards for which no warning or compensation was given. She likened venereal disease to the risk of lead poisoning in a pottery or the danger of combustion in a dynamite factory (C. Hamilton, 1909). Women were forced into marriage, in her view, by the cutting off of any other means of subsistence. They had to surrender their bodies for use in order to be fed and clothed.

Christabel Pankhurst, in the same pre-World War I period in the UK, made a similar connection: 'The system under which a woman must derive her livelihood from her husband – must eat out of his hand as it were – is a great bulwark of sex-subjection, and is a great reinforcement to prostitution. People are led to reason thus: a woman who is a wife is one who has made a permanent sex bargain for her maintenance; the woman who is not married must therefore make a temporary bargain of the same kind' (Pankhurst, quoted in Jackson, 1994, p. 21). The relationship between prostitution and marriage, as two forms of exchange of women for sexual use in return for subsistence, was a fundamental understanding of feminists both in the 'first' and 'second' waves of feminism in the 20th century. Beauvoir made the same point in the 1940s in *The Second Sex*, saying that the wife is 'hired for life by one man; the prostitute has several clients who pay her by the piece. The one is protected by one male against all the others; the other is defended by all against the exclusive tyranny of each' (quoted in Pateman, 1988, p. 190).

A particularly profound critical analysis of marriage was made by Carole Pateman in the mid-1980s (Pateman, 1988). Pateman explains that patriarchy is founded upon the male sex right. This right of men to have sexual access to women's bodies has been most commonly exercised through marriage, and is evidenced by the difficulties feminists have had in getting rape in marriage recognized as a crime instead of as the legitimate exercise of a man's 'conjugal rights'. Men are constructed as individuals and as men through this right: 'The patriarchal construction of sexuality, what it means to be a sexual being, is to possess and to have access to sexual property ... In modern patriarchy, masculinity provides the paradigm for sexuality; and masculinity means sexual mastery. The "individual" is a man who makes use of a woman's body (sexual property); the converse is much harder to imagine' (Pateman, 1988, p. 185). Pateman is clear on the indissoluble connections between marriage and prostitution. As she puts it, 'marriage is now only one of the socially acceptable ways for men to have access to women's bodies' because '[p]rostitution is an integral part of patriarchal capitalism' (ibid., p. 189). Prostitution is also 'part of the exercise of the law of male sex-right, one of the ways in which men are ensured access to women's bodies' (ibid., p. 94). Pateman argues that the 'sexual contract' in which men were awarded and enjoyed possession of subordinate women through their place in a 'brother-hood' of men predated the 'social contact' touted by 17th and 18th century political theorists in the west. As male citizens made 'social contracts' with their governments to be obedient in exchange for good governance, they did so astride the bodies of their already subordinated sisters. Gerda Lerner in the *Creation of Patriarchy* goes further back to look at how patriarchy originated in the ancient Middle East (Lerner, 1987). She identifies the development of the exchange of women for profit as the lynchpin of the developing system of patriarchy. It could, as Pateman observes, take the form either of marriage or of prostitution. The incorporation of the exchange of women for men's sexual use into the fabric of the contemporary global economic system can thus be seen as a logical development that demonstrates and typifies the emergence of capitalism as a patriarchal system in itself. In this understanding prostitution is not peripheral, but central to the current capitalist project.

In the 19th and early 20th centuries feminist campaigners gained legislative changes which allowed women to have some rights in marriage, rather than simply being appendages of husbands who had complete control over their movements and activities (Hollis, 1979). They gained the right to preserve their property and income through the Married Women's Property Acts, some rights to retain custody of their children, and the right to live separately from their husbands, who could previously kidnap escaping wives and lock them up. In 1923 in the UK women obtained the right to divorce on the same grounds as men. The legal basis of marriage in countries with western legal systems has changed considerably. In the late

20th century legislation was changed, or legal precedents established, to make rape in marriage illegal in some countries. This was a crucial development because it established the right of women to control the territory of their bodies and not be simply used at a man's will, but it is comparatively recent. In the vast majority of the world these rights do not exist; wives cannot divorce, for instance, and often do not have freedom of movement. But most importantly for the theme of this chapter, in most jurisdictions women do not have ownership of their bodies in marriage. Husbands may rape them and use them sexually in any way they wish with impunity.

In the west after World War II a new form of marriage which resulted from these legal changes and from women's greater economic opportunities developed, known as 'companionate marriage' (Bernard, 1982). This is widely understood to have abolished the old basis of marriage, which can be seen as servile conditions in which women worked for no pay, husbands had ownership over their bodies and the women had no legal or economic means of escape or redress. Changing relationships between the sexes are understood in the companionate model to have led to a more egalitarian rather than starkly slave owner/slave basis to marriage. The changes which might be expected to lead to progress continue apace, with greater and greater percentages of women entering the workforce in western countries and continuing to work after marriage to create dual-career families. Despite these changes feminist theorists in the 1960s, 1970s and 1980s made very similar arguments to their predecessors about the similarities between marriage and prostitution (Pateman, 1988; Dworkin, 1983).

In fact the traditional elements of marriage have not completely disappeared in western societies, even in the case of employed, highly educated and well paid professional women. The right of men to women's bodies for sexual use has not gone but remains an assumption at the basis of heterosexual relationships in general as a considerable quantity of feminist research reveals (Phillips, 2000). Research on sexual violence in marriage finds that one in seven women who have ever been married has experienced rape with the threat or use of force by husbands (Russell, 1990; Finkelhor and Yllo, 1985). But the research indicates a wider problem for women in relationships with men in the contemporary west, which is that they endure a great deal of unwanted sex, which, though it might not be easily classified as 'rape' since the women do not say no, or even think they have a right to, is often fiercely resented and experienced as profoundly subordinating and abusive (Gavey, 1992; Jeffreys, 1993). In theory these women have the right to leave and may even have the economic resources to do so, though they are likely to suffer reduced living standards. But they feel they have no choice but to stay and endure and may be 'loving to survive' (Graham *et al.*, 1994). Modern marriage and 'marriage-like' heterosexual relationships do not liberate women from the unwanted sex that earlier waves of feminism have criticized so sharply.

'Companionate' marriages, in which there is no direct financial exchange and the woman is apparently in a position to leave, are not the dominant form in the world. The stark reality of traditional patriarchal marriage, as exchange of women between men, is evident in most forms of the practice in the present. In child marriage and arranged/forced marriage women are property exchanged between men. The girls'/women's bodies and labours are owned by their husbands and there is little chance of escape. I choose to use the expression arranged/forced on the grounds that the difference between these forms is sometimes moot (Beckett and Macey, 2001). All these traditional forms of marriage have an economic basis and they include aspects of prostitution, defined as allowing sexual access in return for subsistence, at their heart. The description of women as 'chattels' in the marriage exchange is controversial, however.

Are women bought in marriage?

The question of whether women are bought as if they were chattels or slaves in marriage practices has exercised anthropologists. Valerio Valeri explains that a serious controversy broke out in the journal *Man* in the 1930s over this issue (Valeri, 1994). It seems that the controversy was over the suitability of the term 'bride price'. This was seen as disrespectful and the term 'bride wealth' seems to have won out to describe the money paid by the groom's family to the bride's family at the point where the girl was exchanged. But, Valeri points out, the groom's family in the tribe he studied in Eastern Indonesia quite bluntly speak of buying brides:

> What the anthropologist is taught modestly to call 'bridewealth', they crudely call *mulua heliam* 'the price of the woman'. What he is careful to name the 'prestation' of 'marriage gifts', they name without qualms 'buying the woman'. As if this were not

enough, they shamelessly compare the price of different women and decry the 'priceyness' of some.

(Valeri, 1994, p. 1)

The bride's family, however, calls the transaction 'giving'. Valeri explains that mainstream anthropologists have rejected the idea that 'affinal payments are mere commercial transactions' on the grounds that there are significant differences, such as the fact that a woman cannot be sold on to others by the group that acquires her and the right to 'give her away' remains with the natal group. Valeri is sceptical about these differences and points out that the goods used to buy wives can also be used to buy slaves. Women are more valuable than other goods, he says, because they reproduce and give to the group that buys them 'its existence as a group' (ibid., p. 9). The payment is made because '[i]n giving up a woman as a source of reproduction ... [t]hey must be offered a compensation which they find acceptable'. Moreover the payment made for the bride on marriage is gradually repaid over the lifetime of the marriage. 'There is a clear contrast between the initial stages, when only rights in sexual and culinary access to a woman are transferred, and the later ones, when full control over the woman's residence and her reproductive powers is alienated' (ibid., p. 10).

None of this, however, is likely to make a crucial difference from the wife's point of view. Her body and personhood are exchanged for goods between persons other than herself and she must fulfil the bargain in sexual and reproductive use. In the tribe Valeri studied the husband takes armshells back to the bride's father's house and the rite emphasizes the transfer of the rights in the reproductive potential of the woman to the husband. Another tribe in the same area is even more 'anatomical', as he puts it, with certain types and quantities of valuables being exchanged for different parts of the woman's body, 'a certain type of plate for the skull, a gong for the voice, and so on' (ibid., p. 11).

Bride price or bride wealth are important in determining male authority and rights in relation to the wives who are bought. Thus, in a fascinating study of changing concepts of marriage and the emergence of systems of prostitution in Papua New Guinea, Holly Wardlow (2007) explains how this works:

almost all the men in the study emphasized the importance of bride wealth in determining spouses' obligations to each other and, in part, justifying a man's authority over his wife … Huli men from all generations repeatedly invoked bride wealth as an explanation for why wives were expected to do more agricultural labor than their husbands were, why wives had to ask permission to leave the household, why wives had to comply when a husband requested sexual relations and why wives had to obey a husband's explicit instructions, such as fetching something when asked.

(Wardlow, 2007, p. 1010)

Bride wealth was the basis on which men knew who they could use sexually. A woman for whom bride wealth had been paid belonged to her husband, who had 'sole claim to her sexual and reproductive body' (ibid.).

Gerda Lerner, in her fascinating history of the birth of male dominance in the ancient Middle East, argues that the exchange of women in marriage and the ubiquitous bride price did not mean that women were made into chattels and objects. She says, 'it is not women who are reified and commodified, it is women's sexuality and reproductive capacity which is so treated. The distinction is important. Women never become "things", nor are they so conceived' (Lerner, 1987, p. 212). They did, Lerner tells us, retain their 'power to act'. However, this distinction may be moot. It is hard to separate women's 'sexuality' from their selves, as Carole Pateman (1988) argues. Such a separation would require precisely the mind/body split which lies at the base of contemporary prostitution and proves to be such a damaging aspect thereof (Farley, 2003). Prostituted women have to learn to disassociate their minds from their bodies whilst being used in prostitution, if they have not already learned to do this from experience of child sexual abuse, and those who do not are not able to tolerate the abuse.

Marriage trafficking

A new concern in feminist scholarship about the basis of marriage in women's subordination and the abuses of women's human rights that this involves, has been sparked by the intrusion of traditional forms of servile marriage into the west through the forces of globalization. The clearest example is the mail order bride industry, which involves the acquisition by men of brides from poor countries such as the Philippines or Russia, through commercial agencies which profit from the trade. They may order a bride sight unseen, or they may visit on tours organized by the agencies to select a bride. The proliferation of agencies and the money to be made from this industry now make it a significant player in the international sex industry (Demleitner, 2000). In some cases the women themselves have to pay the agencies in order to have their information displayed, and may even find themselves in debt to the agencies for travel costs, which can be hard to repay if husbands do not allow them access to money. The practice reveals in unalloyed form the traditional basis of marriage, as women's bodies and labour are clearly acquired, in this case by western male owners, in return for subsistence. The UN Trafficking Rapporteur's report for 2007 calls attention to the seriousness of the mail order bride trade as a form of trafficking (UNHRC, 2007a, p.18).

The term 'mail order bride' has been rejected by some feminist commentators for representing women as commodities and being insulting to women who marry in this fashion. Interestingly the same arguments that some feminist scholars have made about other forms of prostitution, i.e. that women's agency or choice should be recognized and that they should not be 'victimized', have been used by feminist commentators in relation to the mail order bride industry. Nora Demleitner, for instance, argues that women who marry in this way are not 'pawns, victims or prostitutes' or 'goods' and should be treated as 'free agents, voluntary actors, highly adventurous, courageous, strong-willed and resourceful individuals' (Demleitner, 2000, p. 626). Nonetheless she characterizes very well the inequality of the relations that mail order brides find themselves in, in terms of economic dependency, lack of language skills and cultural knowledge, isolation from families, friends and all other forms of support, and in constant awareness that if they leave the marriage they may be repatriated and lose any advantage they may have gained out of their experience. The harms appear to include a greater chance of being battered or murdered, and several high profile murder cases in the US in the last decade have placed the spotlight on the abuses women can suffer in such marriages (Terzieff, 2007). As the UN Trafficking Rapporteur, Sigma Huda, points out, this practice is 'incompatible with the equal enjoyment of rights by women and with respect for their rights and dignity. There is an unequal balance of power that puts women at special risk of violence and abuse, particularly when it is the man who is paying money to marry the woman concerned' (UNHRC, 2007a). Often, she explains, mail order bride marriages become 'forced marriages because women are not free to leave because of immigration status, isolation, economic dependence and fear of husbands' (ibid.). There should be no necessary contradiction between recognizing the harms women suffer from male dominance as well as their courage and resourcefulness in dealing with them. Otherwise feminist critique might have to be abandoned altogether on the grounds that it is insulting to women.

The mail order bride industry is the form of marriage most obviously commercialized in the global economy, and the aspect most obviously linked to the global sex industry. The relationship with prostitution is clear, as impoverished women from poor countries give unknown men in whom they have no affectional interest and for whom they have no desire their domestic and reproductive labour and sexual access to their bodies in order to escape from dire economic circumstances. Though mail order bride brokers existed well before the 1990s, the scale and efficiency of the industry may have been restricted by the need to use snail mail. The Internet changed all that: 'When the mail-order bride industry shifted from using a magazine format to operating over the Internet during the 1990s, the number ... providing matchmaking services exploded and spread from Russia and Asia into Latin America' (Schaeffer-Grabiel, 2006, p. 331). One source estimates that the number of companies rose from 200 in 1999 to 500 in 2005, with 4,000–6,000 foreign spouses entering the US each year through the mediation of international marriage brokers (Minnesota Advocates for Human Rights, 2007). The industry is taking root in many rich nations where men seek foreign spouses. Thus there is a considerable industry providing 'wives' from Vietnam and Indonesia for Taiwanese men, for instance (ibid.). Taiwanese men pay agencies up to US$10,000 for trips to China, Indonesia or Vietnam to acquire 'brides'. The number of immigrant spouses in Taiwan is 306,700, accounting for half of the total foreign population in Taiwan. Almost two-thirds are from China and the remaining one-third mostly from South East Asian nations (Tsay, 2004).

Some theorists have identified the development of such practices as emerging from the creation of a 'corporate masculinity' which is being globalized through business practices and connections as well as the Internet. In this 'corporate masculinity', or what Felicity Schaeffer-Grabiel calls, usefully, 'corporate multiculturalism', rich men are able to exercise their male sex right to buy women who are more subordinate than those in their countries of origin, to experience the excitements of exoticism and racist sexual stereotyping, and to cement international relationships through women's bodies. Male western consumers, and particularly businessmen, can all become playboys of the whole world in their access to vulnerable women transnationally. Schaeffer-Grabiel identifies the 'cyberbride' industry as one of the 'transnational routes of U.S. masculinity' (Schaeffer-Grabiel, 2006). In 'corporate multiculturalism' US men seek comparative advantage in the form of being able to buy women's sexual subservience from poor countries in the same way that a US sneaker manufacturer can offshore its production to take advantage of the poverty of Asian workers, mainly women (Enloe, 2004):

> The First World husband is typically looking for a docile, submissive, and subservient bride whom he can control and dominate. He seeks a MOB [mail order bride] specifically because of sexist sentiments, and his hatred and fear of the feminist movement. He rejects women of his own nationality as wives because he considers them to be aggressive and egotistical. He believes they are too ambitious, make excessive demands in marriage, and have expectations of equality with their husbands. He criticizes the desire of women for autonomy, independence, and equality.
>
> (Belleau, 2003, p. 596)

The agency websites regularly solicit custom by promising their male customers that the women they offer will be more subservient than western women. Goodwife.com is a website which provides space for bride agencies to advertise. It states: 'We, as men, are more and more wanting to step back from the types of women we meet now. With many women taking on the "me first" feminist agenda and the man continuing to take a back seat to her desire for power and control many men are turned off by this and look back to having a more traditional woman as our partner' (Goodwife.com, accessed 2008). The site exhibits strong resentment of 'radical feminists' and calls them 'feminazis' 'for their attitudes and position regarding the roles of the man and the woman in a relationship'. These feminists apparently 'want a man to be sensitive to their needs and desires to the point of losing everything about him that makes him a man' (ibid.). The qualities that the Goodwife website identifies as abhorrent in non-traditional wives are the fact that they want to change their husbands, they stop 'taking care' of themselves when they are married, they want to be the 'boss', they provide takeaway food instead of cooking, and they want to work on and improve their relationships with their husbands.

The buying of brides is not just happening in rich countries where regular bride selling agencies have been established. Bride selling as a part of the trafficking of women into sexual exploitation is growing around the world, and particularly in Asia and the Middle East. Wherever women are trafficked as wives they leave the protection of families and friends and the protections offered by being able to speak the language and know the geography far behind. The trade in wives from North Korea to China is a good example. More than 100,000 North Koreans are estimated to have migrated illegally into China in the past decade, with 80–90 per cent of the women becoming trafficking victims (Davis, 2006). The women are trafficked as wives, as prostitutes or start as 'wives' and then find that they are prostituted. The causes of this 'transnational market of selling and exploiting women' lie in both countries (ibid., p. 131). North Korea has experienced severe economic problems since the downfall of the Soviet Union, which used to subsidize the country. Economic output has been halved. Women are vulnerable not just because of economics but because of traditional roles which restrict them to low-level jobs, demand that they leave the workforce when they marry and cut them off from state rations so they become dependent on spouses. As factories shut down women find it harder to get jobs and many see their only option as seeking work in China or marrying a Korean-Chinese or Chinese man so they can help to support their aging parents and other family members. The demand in China comes from the imbalanced sex ratio created by the one-child policy, to the extent that there are 116 males to 110 females. In some regions the imbalance is as high as 14 males to one female. By 2020 it is estimated that there will be more than 40 million bachelors in China looking for wives (ibid.).

Some of the women are trafficked through marriage brokers who promise better lives in China. But the women find their situations are very different from what they were promised. Sometimes the North Korean women are kidnapped whilst trying to migrate and sold into 'marriage' or they are lured by men who say they will find them jobs and then sold, sometimes to farmers who cannot find wives, for anywhere from 400–410,000 yuan (US$50–51,250).

Not only do they suffer violence and severe impoverishment but often they are re-abducted by the brokers or sold by husbands who have tired of them, sometimes ending up being sold multiple times. In one case, a North Korean woman was chained up whenever her Chinese husband left the house to prevent escape (Muico, 2005). One North Korean woman trafficked into forced marriage in China was sold to a 'horrible gambler' who 'offered me to other men as a mortgage' when he ran out of gambling money (ibid., p. 4). The sexual demands of the 'husbands' are experienced as rape: 'the only thing he wanted was for us to always have sex. When I became depressed he beat me ... Every night, he stretched out my arms, tied my wrists and raped me. This hellish life lasted for six months ... When night fell, he appeared, reeking of alcohol, and ruthlessly abused me. He shackled me like a dog so I could not get away'. One woman went to China to look for her eldest daughter who went missing at a border town market in China. She worked as a nanny for a Korean-Chinese family and found that they sold her younger daughter whilst she was running an errand (ibid., p. 5). Sometimes the marriages are more consensual, though the 'brokers' may be the same persons as the 'traffickers' in non-consensual cases. Even those who agree to 'consensual' marriages have no say in who the brokers sell them to. Some of these women too suffer severe sexual and physical violence and imprisonment, though others speak of their 'husbands' being 'kind'.

They cannot escape even if the opportunity arises, because of fear of harsh consequences for themselves and their families in North Korea, where they are treated as criminals if they return, sent to jails, to labour training camps and tortured (ibid.). They may experience forced abortions by drugs or beatings. There have also been cases of infanticide in which other detainees have been forced to participate in the killing of newborns who were left to die, buried alive or suffocated with wet towels because the state did not want more mouths to feed. When women are sent back to their communities they are likely to be treated as social outcasts and thus become vulnerable to re-trafficking. In some cases those who are repatriated are executed as enemies of the state.

In some situations the selling of girls and women for marriage or for prostitution is openly practised. The Asian Human Rights Commission has publicized the sale of girls and women in the Northern Indian states of Rajasthan and Gujarat, for instance (Asian Human Rights Commission, 2007). In Rajasthan girls and women are sold on the open market by their parents on market days just beside the cattle market. The dowry system is implicated here since girl children are seen as a burden when parents cannot afford to pay dowry in order to marry off their daughters and sell them instead. Women and sometimes children are bought and trafficked to various parts of India and to neighbouring countries, mainly for the sex industry. Some are later married and, if not suitable, sold on. A 'fairly beautiful woman' can be bought for as little as US$227. The shortage of women in other areas of India, too, as a result of the selected abortion of unwanted girls, has led to trafficking in wives becoming a blatant and profitable slave buying practice (Huggler, 2006). Sometimes brothers will share a woman, and sometimes beautiful ones are sold on at a profit. In the village of Ghasera, only 40 kilometres from Delhi, there are estimated to be more than 100 trafficked brides. Villagers have attacked police who tried to rescue the brides, and set their cars on fire.

Another form of bride trafficking takes place with the corpses of dead women. In remote areas of China custom demands that unmarried dead sons should be buried with a girl or woman so that he will not be unhappy (Fremson, 2006). Not only is sex-selective abortion affecting the chance men have of marrying but also women leave for the cities, never to return. They do not want to remain in the privation of a rural lifestyle. Families rely on agents to find dead daughters that can be bought to share the graves of sons. Parents see this as a duty to their daughters too, who must be married even if they are dead because, according to a Beijing sociology professor, 'China is a paternal clan culture. A woman does not belong to her parents. She must marry and have children of her own before she has a place among her husband's lineage. A woman who dies unmarried has no place in this world' (ibid.).

The difference between prostitution in brothels or on the street and forced marriages brokered by traffickers resides mainly in the number of men that the woman is sexually used by. In 'marriage' there are usually fewer than in prostitution. One factor common to the experience of women who are subject to marriage trafficking through US agencies or by being kidnapped is that they will have to accept sexual use by a man in whom they are most likely to have no erotic interest. Like other women who are prostituted, they will have to learn to disassociate their minds from their bodies to bear the sexual assaults they suffer in return for subsistence. This feature is likely to be common to the experience of women in other forms of forced marriage too, which are taking place in western countries in immigrant communities.

Forced marriage

The UN Working Group on Contemporary Forms of Slavery recognized in 2003 that forced marriage is a form of contemporary slavery, a form of trafficking and a form of sexual exploitation (UNHRC, 2007a). The 1956 Supplementary Convention on the Abolition of Slavery that the working group monitors includes within its definition of slavery any institution or practice whereby '[a] woman, without the right to refuse, is promised or given in marriage on payment of a consideration in money or in kind to her parents, guardian, family or any other person or group'. It extends to situations where '[t]he husband of a woman, his family or his clan, has the right to transfer her to another person for value received or otherwise' and where '[a] woman on the death of her husband is liable to be inherited by another person'. It also includes child marriage in the clause identifying as slavery '[a]ny institution or practice whereby a child or young person under the age of 18 years, is delivered by either or both of his natural parents or by his guardian to another person, whether for reward or not, with a view to the exploitation of the child or young person or of his labour'. Unfortunately little progress has been made on this issue and in some countries child marriage is on the rise.

It is interesting to note that the UN Trafficking Rapporteur's report casts doubt on the possibility of easily making a distinction between forced and arranged marriage: 'The Special Rapporteur is concerned that in some cases the difference between an arranged and a forced marriage is tenuous' (UNHRC, 2007a, p. 26). This problem of making a distinction has been commented upon by many feminist scholars in recent years, which have seen a moderation in the way arranged marriage has traditionally been defended by 'progressive' scholars, i.e. on cultural relativist grounds which involve recognizing the practices of another culture as legitimate without value judgement (Beckett and Macey, 2001; Moschetti, 2006). The problems inherent in arranged marriage and its connections with forced marriage have come under scrutiny because of an increasing rejection by feminist theorists and activists of 'harmful cultural practices' and a developing critique of forms of multiculturalism in theory and practice that defend or promote them (Okin, 1999; Nussbaum, 2000).

Nonetheless state agencies, such as the Home Office in the UK, and many feminist scholars who are well aware of the severe harms of forced marriage do still seek to differentiate it from arranged marriage. Anne Phillips and Moira Dustin, for instance, in an article in which they most usefully outline the UK policy responses to the problem of forced marriage in the British Asian community, argue that 'arranged' marriage may be more successful than 'romantic' marriage and gloss over the aspects of arranged marriage which are related to prostitution. They say that 'research that parents carry out on potential partners may well prove a better guide to future compatibility than the more haphazard mechanisms of dating; and the expectations attached to arranged marriage may be more realistic than those associated with "romantic" marriage' (Phillips and Dustin, 2004, p. 540). They do not mention the problem that the bride will have to submit her body to sexual use by someone she does not know, or scarcely knows, and may have no liking for, let alone desire. Differentiation between arranged and forced marriages is difficult when the degree of non-physical force that may be employed to persuade a girl to accept her parents' wishes is taken into account, such as the real threat of ostracism from the extended family or the possibility of physical retribution. Jasvinder Sanghera runs an organization in the UK to help girls and women who are escaping arranged marriages, and her book *Shame*, based on the experiences of her sisters and herself, is most instructive on the kinds of pressures that are used (Sanghera, 2007). Cultural relativist arguments are still being made, too, in the justice systems of western countries, with disastrous results. In Australia there has been considerable public outcry in recent years when cultural relativist arguments have been used by judges in the courts to hand down extremely light penalties for old aboriginal men who have, in continuance of a traditional harmful practice, taken possession of young teenage girls 'promised' by their parents since early childhood, and subjected them to brutal rapes (Moschetti, 2006).

In the UK the practice of arranged marriage, and support for the custom, is falling substantially in younger generations of the Pakistani, Bangladeshi and Indian communities in which it has been most commonly practised. Some parents, however, are turning to forced marriage to deal with the problems of independence, drug use and crime that their children are exhibiting (Phillips and

Dustin, 2004). Girls are trafficked by their parents to the country in which the family has its origins, often on the pretext of taking a holiday to meet the relatives, and abandoned with a man to whom they are forcefully married off. Increasingly there has been a recognition of the link between the number of 'honour killings' that are taking place in the UK and arranged/forced marriages. Families are murdering their daughters in order to prevent the shame that would result from the girl's rejection of an arranged marriage or her determination to date a boy of her choice (Welchman and Hossain, 2005). In response, there has been a flurry of government concern, with a Home Office inquiry, special instructions to police forces and other social services, a plan to legislate against forced marriages (later rejected), and the setting up of squads and units in the Foreign Office and the police force to counter the problem. The Foreign Office unit, which is responsible for identifying and supporting young people who reside in the UK but have gone 'missing' after taking holidays on the Indian subcontinent, handles 250–300 cases yearly (Phillips and Dustin, 2004).

In some cases husbands or wives in arranged/forced marriages are imported to the UK. Thus in 2000 over 10,000 Pakistani nationals obtained entry clearance to join spouses in the UK. The practice of British-born children marrying Pakistani nationals is increasing. Most weddings take place in Pakistan, after which the husband or wife applies for permission to come to the UK. Until 1997 most of these migrants were women. In 1997 the 'Primary Purpose Rule', which refused entry to spouses who were suspected of using marriage as a way to immigrate, was abolished. Thereafter the numbers of husbands gaining entry has increased to almost equal proportions. The marriages offer parents in the UK a way to 'strengthen connections between much-missed kin separated by migration decades earlier' (Charsley, 2005, p. 86). The marriages are consanguineous, i.e. carried out between cousins or other close kin, which is in contrast to the practice of consanguineous marriage tending to die out in other societies. Whilst there are serious problems for young girls imported into UK families in such arranged marriages, in that they are entirely without recourse should their husbands be violent and bullying, the girls who wed immigrant husbands may suffer severely too. The men may be using marriage as a way to obtain visas and be intending to abandon their wives. Their frustrations at not being in a position of power in their own families relative to their brides may cause them to be violent (ibid.).

Some arranged marriages in immigrant communities are actually 'child' marriages, taking place before the legally acceptable age. In the UK, Germany and Australia, some women from particular immigrant communities are being married off by their parents to men they do not choose at young ages, and in some cases are being sent overseas to be traded off as child brides in Lebanon or Pakistan, a practice that is hard to distinguish from other forms of trafficking for sexual exploitation. Direct monetary exchange is often involved as the girls are exchanged for bride price or dowry. Some fathers from the Lebanese community in Australia traffic their daughters to Lebanon, where they are married to relatives at ages from 14 upwards (Harris, 2005). The girls do not know the purpose of the visits. Some manage to get to the Australian embassy, demanding to be returned home. In one case that was reported in the media a 14-year-old girl turned up at the embassy with her suitcases saying she had been married against her will at 13 and imprisoned. In 2005 embassy staff reported that they had handled 12 cases in two years of teenagers fleeing arranged marriages, of which 7 involved minors, (ibid.). Social workers estimated that there were several hundred cases yearly of girls dropping out of school to get married, mainly in Sydney and Melbourne. It would be wrong, however, to see child marriage as a problem only of communities who do not ascribe to Christian values. The Trafficking Rapporteur's report points to evidence that adolescent girls are trafficked over the border between polygamous communities in the US and in Canada in order to enter into arranged polygamous marriages (UNHRC, 2007a). Child marriage in immigrant communities in western countries, however, does not take place on the very considerable scale that it does in Asia and Africa.

Child marriage

The UN Trafficking Rapporteur's report argues that the practice of child marriage should be understood as a form of trafficking in women (UNHRC, 2007a). The 1964 marriage convention defines child marriage as forced marriage which must be strictly prohibited, because children are incapable of consent. It fits the definition of slavery in the slavery convention very well since the child is completely within the control of her owner/husband. Unfortunately international instruments are inadequate to deal with the problem. There is no recommended minimum age of marriage identified in the marriage convention. The Convention on the Rights of the Child defines childhood as the period before the age of 18 but marriage is understood to officially remove the child from this category and in most jurisdictions the legal age of marriage for girls is below 18. It is possible that it is the very importance of marriage as the basis of the social organization of male dominance that bedevils the task of ending the practice (Moschetti, 2006). Marriage is treated with unreasonable respect and trumps all protections that children might otherwise have recourse to. Nonetheless human rights activists and researchers on child marriage take as their understanding of 'the child' young persons under 18 years old in accordance with the Convention on the Rights of the Child 1989 (CRC).

The sexual use that children are subjected to in marriage might be characterized either as rape or as prostitution, and has severely harmful effects on the physical and mental wellbeing of the girls involved. In Purna Sen's research in Calcutta, for instance, almost half of the women in her sample had been married at or below the age of 15, and the youngest was merely seven years old. One woman explained that her marriage at 14 to a previously married man was precipitated by her parents finding blood on her clothes from an injured goat she had carried home. Since it was assumed that she had started to menstruate she was married off three months later. She described her husband's sexual use of her thus: 'It was very bad, very difficult. I had a lot of pain … I used to be scared when he came to get me and carry me to his bed. I used to cry and go to lie somewhere else, but he'd come and get me' (Ouattara et al., 1998, p 30).

The numbers of girls involved in child marriages are considerable (Bunting, 2000). The estimated percentages of girls married at very young ages vary between countries. In Cameroon, for instance, 62 per cent of girls are married before the legal minimum age of 18 (Mathur et al., 2003). Worldwide there are 51 million girls between 15 and 19 years who are married. In West Africa, South Asia, East and Central Africa 30 per cent or more of girls aged 15–19 are already married. The percentage of girls who are married before age 18 in Niger is 82 per cent, in Bangladesh 75 per cent, in Nepal 63 per cent, in India 57 per cent and in Uganda 50 per cent. The number of girls who are expected to marry before 18 in the decade after 2003 is 100,000,000. The International Centre for Research on Women's report on child marriage comments on the significance of the commercial element in these marriages: 'in most cultures around the world, economic transactions are integral to the marriage process, with an underlying assumption that these costs are lower when marriage occurs at an early age' (ibid., p. 5). Dowry is an important cause of the continuing low age of marriage, because dowries are lowest when the girls are young and seen as most valuable, and increase as they grow older, so for impoverished parents it is imperative to marry off their daughters early. In relation to bride price the report comments that 'it is when a girl is young that her productive labor and reproductive capacities are seen as "best buys" in exchange for valued cattle or other goods' (ibid., p. 6). The term 'child' marriage should perhaps be seen as a euphemism because this practice is gendered, and it is overwhelmingly girls and not boys who are subjected to it. The difference is stark, since in Mali the girl:boy ratio of marriage before age 18 is 72:1, in Kenya, 21:1, and even in the United States it is 8:1 (Nour, 2006).

Worsening economic conditions through wars, drought or the destruction of subsistence lead to an increase in the marriage trafficking of girls as fathers decide to relieve themselves of the burden of feeding their girl children and, where bride price exists, make a profit from selling them. Though the international human rights community is in some agreement that progress has been made in the last decade in reducing child marriage, where certain exigencies exist the reverse is the case. Thus in Afghanistan increased child marriage is the result of the privations suffered through the last decade of conflict. The Afghanistan Independent Human Rights Commission estimates that 57 per cent of marriages involve girls under the legal marriage age of 16 (IRIN, 2007). Though the government has introduced a new marriage contract to combat child marriage which decrees that marriage certificates cannot be issued for brides under 16, this is unlikely to be effective when the vast majority of 'marriages' are not officially registered. But it is not just poverty that causes child marriage. The practice originates in the desire to get girls married before they can be sexually used and thus lose the virginity which guarantees a good bride price, and the family's honour (Bunting, 2000).

In her work on child marriage, Annie Bunting provides a very useful warning to human rights activists not to imagine that child marriage is a problem of non-western cultures (Bunting, 2000). She points out that early sexualization of girls in the west is a significant problem that results in similar harms to girls such as early pregnancies and truncated education. The men who sexually use young teenage girls in the US, for instance, are routinely 10 years older than the girls and engaged in what should be seen as child abuse. The reaction of state welfare and justice systems can be quite different, however. They may waive penalties if the men marry the girl children, who may be 13 or 14 years old, and they may even encourage such marriages, particularly if the girls are pregnant Latinas, to relieve the welfare system of extra mouths to feed. The implication of Bunting's argument is that the campaign against child marriage needs to be widened to include the sexual use of girl children at early ages whether they are married or not.

Temporary marriage

Marriage of underage girls is taking place in some Muslim communities in Yemen and Egypt in a form in which the elements of prostitution are most clearly represented. The practice is called 'temporary marriage' and parents sell the girls for short-time sexual use by rich foreign Muslim men (IRIN, 2005, 2006). In other countries the women involved are likely to be adults and taking part in the practice out of dire economic need, or they may be divorcees or women who have no other way to support their children. This is practised by Shi'a Muslims in the Middle East. It is defended by some Muslim scholars as having been engaged in by Mohamed himself and as necessary particularly for men who travel for business or study and need a temporary sexual outlet (Haeri, 1992). It is promoted as being a protection against prostitution, and even as good for women since it can be a way that poor women and widows can gain some subsistence. Temporary marriages are solemnized before clerics and last for anything from a couple of hours to a lifetime. In Iran the practice of sigheh is being touted by clerics as a solution to the permissiveness that the clerical régime sees as developing in the country. Thus in 1990 Ali Akbar Hashemi Rafsanjani gave a sermon whilst he was president of Iran advising that temporary marriage was a religiously acceptable alternative to western promiscuity. This led to a storm of protest from women because the practice is so clearly about men's rights. A married man can have as many temporary wives as he wants, as well as up to four permanent ones, and can break the contract any time he wants, whereas women cannot. Women who are married 'temporarily' are seen as no longer virgins and have little chance of permanent marriage. They do not have the same rights to inheritance and support when the marriage ends, and neither do any children of the union. There are tens of thousands of children of temporary marriages whose fathers do not acknowledge them and who are therefore considered illegitimate. As recently as 2007 Iran's Interior Minister, Mostafa Pour-Mohammadi, promoted temporary marriage as a solution to the country's social problems (Harrison, 2007). Temporary marriage is now being exploited by the prostitution tourism industry, with a travel agent in Tehran advertising holidays by the Caspian Sea for couples wanting to have temporary marriages, with accommodation and a cleric to solemnize the marriage (ibid.).

There has been a rise in temporary marriages in Iraq, which is worrying women's rights campaigners who say that 300 occur daily in the three main cities in the south of the country, Kerbala, Najaf and Basra, the main Shi'ite cities. The phenomenon is explained as resulting from the poverty suffered by women, especially those who have lost their husbands during the years of war. They seek to protect their children and feed them. As Salua Fatihi, head of two non-governmental women's rights organizations, puts it: 'They [men] use them as sexual objects under the guise of a religious belief' (WLUML, 2006). A payment, often around US$1,000 or the equivalent in gold, is made to the woman. The practice was banned during Saddam Hussein's régime but has re-emerged since 2003. As one woman whose husband had died in the war said of her experience of the practice: 'I was his sexual slave for one month and then he just said my time had expired and left' (ibid.). Another woman was used sexually for a week and the man left her pregnant, with the result that she is now seen as a prostitute. One cleric who presided over five such marriages a day in Najaf explained that the practice protected women's honour and was helpful to them because they could support their families (ibid.).

In some countries where temporary marriage is practised it more closely resembles child prostitution and the girls are directly sold by their parents. Saudi men, for instance, buy access to teenage girls in Yemen in this fashion (IRIN, 2005). Low incomes encourage parents to sell their daughters to men from the Gulf States, who use them sexually for a month or so in a hotel and then abandon them. Forty-two per cent of Yemen's 19.7 million people live on under US$2 per day. According to the UN World Food Programme 7.9 per cent of people in Yemen experience severe food insecurity and cannot afford to buy food for themselves or their family. Once the girls have been abandoned they are stigmatized as divorcees and unlikely to remarry. This form of 'sex tourism' temporary marriage also takes place in Egypt, where girls as young as 14 are sold to Saudi men (IRIN, 2006).

Conclusion

This chapter has sought to show that prostitution is less a legitimate form of women's work than a harmful cultural practice which cannot be easily differentiated from traditional forms of marriage in which women are exchanged between men for cash or other advantages. Human rights instruments and campaigners seek to eliminate forced and child marriage, rather than normalizing them. The progress of women's equality requires that the elements of prostitution are removed from marriage, so that no women have to accept sexual use of their bodies which is against their inclinations. The future of women's equality does not have a place for either servile marriage or the industry of prostitution which places precisely this traditional abuse of women's physical autonomy and exercise of the male sex right in the marketplace. Unfortunately, as we shall see in Chapter 3, the ability to recognize prostitution as a harmful practice has been undermined by the growth and influence of the pornography industry in western countries. Pornography creates an acceptance that the practice of prostitution is acceptable and even enjoyed by the women who are used. It transforms traditional cultures as this western practice creates new markets for sexual exploitation.

Chapter 3

The international political economy of pornography

The pornography industry is the launching pad of the contemporary normalization of the sex industry in the west. It is where the considerable growth throughout the sector began. Defended in the counterculture and sexual revolution of the 1970s as 'transgressive' and liberating (Jeffreys, 1990/91), it is now a massively profitable industry which has been mainstreamed to provide revenue for major corporations. The foundation of the industry is the sexual use of girls and young women made vulnerable by homelessness and histories of sexual abuse, or by trafficking. But the profits of this industry do not flow to those who are most harmed by it. The harms have been made invisible as pornography has been normalized within popular culture, through the entertainment, sports, music and fashion industries (Jeffreys, 2005). Pornography has made the sex industry hip. It has created customers for strip clubs, sometimes called 'live pornography', and ultimately for brothels and other forms of prostitution. The doubling in the percentage of men in the UK in 10 years who now prostitute women has been attributed to the normalization of the commercial sexual exploitation of women that pornography and strip clubs have enabled (Ward and Day, 2004). In this chapter I will examine the expansion and globalization of the industry, and what is involved in its production.

Feminist theory and pornography

In the mid-1980s the feminist opposition to pornography was at its height, and provided a motivating force to the women's liberation movement. This opposition developed in response to the decensorship of pornography that took place in the so-called sexual revolution of the 1960s and 1970s (Jeffreys, 1990/91).

Feminist critics rejected the normalizing impulses that represented pornography as just sex or representation, and any attempts to limit its production as 'censorship' and a threat to free speech. They argued that pornography provided the DNA of male dominance, and Kathleen Barry described pornography as the propaganda of womanhatred (Barry, 1979). It was seen as violence against women because of what was done to the girls and women in the production of pornography, and it was understood to provide men with a roadmap for sexual violence against women, teaching them to see women as loving and deserving of abuse (Dworkin, 1981). In the mid-1980s it looked as if the feminist opposition might bear fruit in the anti-pornography ordinance drawn up in the US by radical feminist theorists Andrea Dworkin and Catharine MacKinnon, which allowed women a civil remedy against pornographers. Women harmed in the making of pornography or by having it used against them could sue the makers and distributors of the materials (MacKinnon and Dworkin, 1997). But, to the devastation of many of those campaigning against pornography, a feminist defence of the practice developed, which echoed precisely the arguments of male free speech liberals and the male manufacturers, that it was a form of 'speech' which must be defended lest censorship be allowed to chill political freedom in America (MacKinnon, 1993). The ordinance was successfully challenged by an alliance of civil liberties groups and feminists who adopted a free speech approach, and it was never implemented.

In the mid- to late 1980s feminist communities and activism in the west were riven by what some called the 'sex wars', in which feminist anti-violence feminists who opposed the sexual exploitation of women and demanded the total transformation of the dominant/submissive sexuality of male supremacy were vigorously resisted by others who promoted a 'sexual freedom' which took as its foundation the very sexuality that male power had created (Jeffreys, 1990/91). The fissure between these different perspectives on sexuality was so wide, and the sexual freedom camp so powerfully underpinned by male liberals and pornographers in mainstream media and culture, that feminist anti-pornography campaigning had by the 1990s lost its momentum. Thus the transformation of pornography into a hugely profitable and mainstream industry sector in the 1990s was able to take place with little interruption from the pickets and protests that characterized the previous two decades.

The work of Laura Kipnis, who teaches Radio-TV-Film at Northwestern University, is a good example of the sexual freedom/free speech approach (Kipnis, 2003). Her enthusiastic defence of pornography is quite far reaching. She does not look at pornography as an industry, or notice that anything is done to real live women and girls in the production of it. She sees pornography as 'fantasy' and an essential part of 'culture': 'Pornography *is* a form of cultural expression, and though it's transgressive, disruptive, and hits below the belt – in more ways than one – it's an essential form of contemporary national culture' (ibid., p. viii). The argument that proponents of pornography are in some way countercultural is rather thin considering the way that pornography has been mainstreamed into western culture, but some still cling to the romantic notion that pornographers are 'transgressive' in using or defending the practice, rather than simply the flag bearers of male dominance. The opponents of pornography, in Kipnis' view, 'seem universally overcome by a leaden, stultifying literalness, apparently never having heard of metaphor, irony, a symbol – even fantasy seems too challenging a concept' (ibid., p. 163). Feminist attacks on pornography, she says, are 'so depressing and so politically problematic' (ibid., p. 188). The feminist critics are, she considers, middle class and inhibited, wanting to 'annihilate' the 'low-rent *Hustler* male and his pleasures' (ibid., p. 148). Feminists should not worry because '*Hustler*'s "violations" are symbolic' and have no connection to 'real sex or violence' (ibid., p. 158). There are no real live women being sexually exploited and abused in the 'fantasy' porn that Kipnis defends.

Nadine Strossen, President of the American Civil Liberties Union and a law professor, takes a similar approach. She is dedicated to defending 'free speech', and calls pornography 'sexual expression' which it is vital to defend from censors (Strossen, 2000). The women's movement, she claims, depends on 'robust free expression, particularly in the realm of sexuality' (ibid., p. 29). She is even more dismissive of feminist concerns: 'It is essential to derail the traditionalist-feminist antisex-juggernaut before its impact on public perceptions and public policy becomes even more devastating' (ibid., p. 29). Clearly, to American liberals the feminist opposition to pornography did seem powerful, though it was unable to limit or dent the growth of the industry. However, in the 21st century there is evidence of a revival in feminist activism and concern about pornography, in response to the size and influence of the industry and the way that it is seen to be constructing the culture in which women, and particularly young women, live (Levy, 2005; Paul, 2005; Guinn and DiCaro, 2007; Stark and Whisnant, 2004).

In contradiction to this free speech approach, Catharine MacKinnon, both before and after the untimely death of Andrea Dworkin in 2005, has continued to point out that pornography is not *Only Words* (MacKinnon, 1993), but a political practice that subordinates women. It is an essential and inseparable part of the industry of prostitution and a form of trafficking in women for sexual exploitation. As she explains: 'In material reality, pornography is one way women and children are trafficked for sex. To make visual pornography, the bulk of the industry's products, real women and children, and some men, are rented out for use in commercial sex acts. In the resulting materials, these people are then conveyed and sold for a buyer's sexual use' (MacKinnon, 2006, p. 247). Pornography is a 'technologically sophisticated slave traffic' allowed 'because its victims are regarded as socially worthless' (ibid., p. 112). Pornography may be a particularly severe form of prostitution in terms of the harms that the women prostituted in this practice experience. This chapter will address the harms of the production process as well as testing out more generally the view that pornography is about harmless fantasy and 'speech' and socially 'transgressive'.

The worth of the industry

The size and worth of the pornography industry in the present, and the extent to which it has been mainstreamed into the day to day business of major corporations and into the entertainment, music and fashion industries (Jeffreys, 2005), should immediately cast doubt on any notion that pornography is 'transgressive', though this is an idea that its defenders still cling to. The industry is now covered seriously in the business pages of newspapers. Pornography companies, such as Beate Uhse from Germany, are listed on the Stock Exchange. The exact profits being made from the industry are hard to gauge, partly because there is such a diversity of forms of sexual exploitation involved, and because some companies are not keen for their involvement in pornography to be known. Frederick Lane's book *Obscene Profits* (2001) provides useful information on the history and *modus operandi* of the industry. It is also a good example of the extent to which the industry has become respectable since it is a 'how-to' book for aspiring pornography entrepreneurs published by a mainstream academic publisher, Routledge. As he chattily explains: 'As the pornography industry continues to grow increasingly mainstream, the social barriers for starting an adult business will continue to drop' (Lane, 2001, p. 146). Lane is surprisingly frank, in his very positive account of the industry, about the fact that it is controlled by men and the profits go to men. Thus, he explains: 'While the number of sites actually run by women is certainly higher than two, it probably is not significantly higher … The images of women and the profits they generate are still largely controlled by men … the demand is being satisfied by the sale of large collections of photographs of women who were paid a nominal amount (if at all)' (Lane, 2001, p. 211). Lane estimated that in 2001 the total worth of the industry in the US was US$10 billion or possibly as much as $15–20 billion (Lane, 2001, p. xiv). Even using the most conservative estimate, he explains, the pornography industry takes in about what Americans pay for sporting events and live musical performances combined.

In 2007 a website which reviews technology for the web, including Internet filter systems, Top Ten Reviews, collated information from a number of sources on the size and worth of the pornography industry. Pornography revenue for the US was estimated at $13.33 billion, which is higher than the total revenue of the media corporations ABC, NBC and CBS. Top Ten Reviews estimated that the industry was worth US$97.06 billion worldwide, which is more than the combined revenue of the top ten web technology companies such as Microsoft, Google and Amazon (Top Ten Reviews, 2007). In 2007 there were 4.2 million porn websites, which constituted 12 per cent of all websites, and 420 million web pages of pornography. Internet sales of porn were estimated to be worth $4.9 billion. By country, the largest number of pornography webpages originated in the US, with 244,661,900, followed by Germany, with 10,030,200, the UK, with 8,506,800, Australia, with 5,655,800, Japan, with 2,700,800, the Netherlands, with 1,883,800, Russia, with 1,080,600, Poland, with 1,049,600, and Spain, with 852,800. In Denmark pornography is estimated to be the third largest industry in financial terms, and Richard Poulin points out that the country was the cradle of the 'sexual revolution' which decensored pornography and ushered in the commercialization of women's sexual subordination (Poulin, 2005, p. 108). European Internet users paid 70 per cent of the US$364 million they spent in 2001 on pornography (ibid.). The number of hardcore pornography titles produced increased from 1,300 in 1988 to 12,000 in 2004 and 13,588 in 2005 (Top Ten Reviews, 2007). The big mainstream pornography distribution companies had considerable incomes. Playboy earned US$331,100,000 in 2006, for instance, and Beate Uhse earned US$271 million.

The part of the industry that resides in the San Fernando Valley in Hollywood was estimated to be worth US$1 billion in 2006 (Barrett, 2007). This is the main area of production in the US and has 200 companies operating. In 15 years the Valley's 'adult entertainment' industry has quadrupled, with annual revenues equal to the restaurant, fast-food and bar businesses in the area combined (ibid.). The studios are mostly small and the movies cheap to make, most costing $20,000 or less. However, Vivid, the Valley's biggest company, made US$150 million in 2005. The average production worker makes $61,000 per year. The Californian industry employs 20,000 and pays US$31 million in taxes just on the sale of videos (Poulin, 2005). Changes are taking place in the industry, though, which threaten its profit base. Sales and rentals of X-rated DVDs were down 15 per cent in 2006 because Internet competition is reducing the market (ibid.). Most of the money in the pornography industry in the US is made by the distributors, such as pay-per-view and subscription porn businesses, cable and satellite companies, adult channels and hotels, which are worth US$1.7 billion (ibid.). In the American hotel system, 40 per cent of rooms have pay-per-view pornography, which accounts for 50 per cent of the videos watched. This is worth $200 million per year (ibid.). The considerable profits of the pornography industry need to be weighed against the financial pain suffered by the male consumers. A 2008 study by the UK Insolvency Helpline found that a quarter of people, overwhelmingly male, with problem debt confessed to spending money on viewing pornography, phone sex and visiting brothels or strip clubs (Chivers, 2008). The sex industry, the report concludes, lies in third place behind drug and alcohol abuse and shopping addiction in the table of the most common reasons for getting into debt. Some men lost their jobs because of their 'sex obsessions' and this male behaviour also led to divorce, which deepened their financial problems.

Phone sex is another lucrative aspect of the pornography industry. Frederick Lane suggested that in 2000 phone sex alone generated between $750 million and $1 billion in revenues in the US, with as much as 50 per cent being retained by US long-distance telephone carriers (Lane, 2001, p. 151). Impoverished Third World nations gain income from having lax phone regulations and high per-minute phone rates that US customers are charged for placing calls to those countries. Thus, according to Lane, the island of São Tomé saw the number of calls it received from the US go from 4,300 in 1991 to 360,000 in 1993. The island kept approximately $500,000 of the $5.2 million worth of phone sex calls and used the money to build a new telecommunications system (ibid.). Not only is the work very low paid but even Lane, who is so positive generally about the pornography industry, admits that crank callers and 'misogynists' can create problems for the women employed. Not surprisingly, the average burnout rate is six months. The women workers, he explains, make an average of US$9–10 per hour, while bureaux get US$180–360. The workers are, he says, 'mostly undereducated and single mums' (ibid.).

Expansion of the industry

The forces that enabled the pornography industry to develop from a marginal activity, a secret men's business of stag films shown at private parties, to the mainstream industry of today included changes in government and community attitudes and technological developments. In the 1960s and 1970s in western countries censorship controls on pornography were progressively relaxed under the influence of the 'sexual revolution'. Pornography was represented as embodying sexual freedom. I have argued elsewhere that this sexual revolution simply enshrined as positive social values men's rights of sexual access to women as playthings in pornography and prostitution and in their sexual relationships (Jeffreys, 1990/91, 1997). Certainly women made some gains. Women's rights to some form of sexual response and to have sexual relationships outside marriage became much more accepted, but the main beneficiary of this 'revolution', I suggest, is the international sex industry.

According to Frederick Lane, the period 1957–73 is referred to in the business as the 'Golden Age of Porn'. He explains that the industry was stimulated by the demand of American soldiers in World War II for 'girlie mags'. Thus the military prostitution which was such a force in the construction of prostitution and sex tourism industries in South East Asia after World War II was involved in constructing the global sex industry in another arena too. When the war ended the magazines were launched onto the US home market. *Playboy* was founded in 1953 and launched on the Stock Exchange in 1971. *Hustler* was founded in 1974. The Playboy company was able to exploit a different form of male bonding, substituting businessmen in this economic boom period for the military. Lane explains that the Playboy clubs were set up to service 'businessmen' who were 'looking for ways to tangibly reward themselves for their success' (Lane, 2001, p. 26). They found this in 'holding a key to a Playboy Club', which was a 'tangible symbol of having "made it"' (ibid.). As Lane records: 'The clubs were a huge success; in the last quarter of 1961, for instance, more than 132,000 people visited the Chicago night club, making it the busiest in the world at the time' (ibid.). In this period it was expensive to produce pornography, so the industry was dominated by the few production companies that could afford the US$200,000–300,000 needed to make one film. In the 'Golden Age' the mafia-controlled industry made links with free speech activists and developed the money and resources to fight legal cases to protect their industry against attempts to restrict it.

In the 1980s and 1990s the sex industry was able to expand in an economic and social climate of *laissez-faire*, free market individualism. The political liberalism associated with this particular economic ideology privileged men's 'free speech' right to pornography over the rights of women to physical integrity. The expansion was facilitated by the development of new technologies such as the video cassette and the Internet. The video cassette recorder (VCR) was born in 1973 and was a crucial technology for pornography because it provided privacy for the male consumers. They could access pornography without having to go to special theatres or peep shows. Pornography drove the video revolution, leading to the explosion of adult video stores and eventually mainstream chains such as Blockbuster. In the early 1990s the development of the Internet provided the pornography industry with important new opportunities. It was easier for the male consumers to protect their anonymity, and they did not have to leave their homes to visit the video store.

Hardcore pornography went mainstream with the release of *Deep Throat* in 1972. Linda Lovelace, the prostituted woman in the movie who had penises thrust down her throat with the justification that she had a clitoris there, was controlled by a violent pimp/husband and her bruises were visible on screen (Lovelace, 1987). Her sexual slavery is generally agreed to be the moment the modern industry took off. 'Adult' movies stopped being a dirty little secret and became part and parcel of the entertainment mainstream. Frank Sinatra put on a showing of *Deep Throat* for US Vice President Agnew at his home (Adult Video News, 2002). The American talk show host Johnny Carson joked about the film on *The Tonight Show* in the early 1970s. Reporters Woodward and Bernstein in the Watergate scandal dubbed their informant 'Deep Throat'.

The easy accessibility of consumer camcorders in the late 1970s led to homemade pornography. Amateur pornography led to what is now known as gonzo porn, which is created by the male actor holding the camera himself and interspersing the sexual use of women with interviews with them. The development of digital technologies made it possible for men to market their female partners straight onto the Internet, cutting out the middleman. Pornography became more easily accessible in the mid-1990s as its reach extended to cable and satellite systems, allowing consumers to purchase adult videos without even having to leave their home. It was at this stage that the pornography industry became attractive to corporate America, to General Motors and AT&T. The new delivery systems enabled blue-chip corporations to profit from pornography without getting too close to the product. In the mid-1990s extreme hardcore pornography became popular amongst young men. This included such practices as 'spit and gape', where a man would stretch his partner's anus as wide as it would go and place a speculum and hose into it in which he could spit or urinate. Anal and double penetration became requirements and what was known in the industry as the 'airtight' trick, meaning a penis in every orifice, gang rape, what is called 'choke-fucking', and bukkake, in which 50–80 men ejaculate simultaneously onto the naked body of a woman lying on the ground.

The mainstream pornography industry went very quickly from being disreputable to gaining very considerable social acceptability in the 1990s. Adult Video News (AVN) attributes the expansion of the industry in this period to the policy of the Clinton administration not to prosecute pornography (Adult Video News, 2002). AVN speculates that Clinton was a libertine who liked pornography and had a special stock on his aeroplane Air Force One (ibid.). In this period the number of pornography production companies doubled and pornography made inroads into many areas of American society. The US industry went to great efforts to gain acceptance, such as hiring lobbyists, participating in charity and campaigning for condom use to prevent HIV infection. It learned from another very harmful industry, tobacco, which, though it has lost social standing now, at one time used lobbyists and spokespersons to front for the industry very well. The Marlboro men were used to promote the industry, for instance, though some died of its effects.

Donna Hughes (2000) identifies the US as the 'country mainly responsible for the industrialization of pornography and prostitution' through local and military prostitution and through the development of an unregulated Internet pornography industry. She points out that the US 'set the policy for the commercial development of the Internet' through Ira Magaziner, Senior Advisor to the President for Policy Development 1993–8. Magaziner coordinated government strategy on electronic commerce and the digital economy, advocating for a free market policy towards the Internet, where the private sector led the development and regulation of the new technology. He said that the lack of governmental interference gave rise to 50 per cent of the economic growth of the US economy in the seven to eight years before 1999. He argued that censorship would be impossible, and problems with pornography such as the protection of privacy and protecting children could be dealt with by empowering people to protect themselves and the placing of responsibility on parents to protect their children from harm. Such protection, he said, was not a role for government. This policy gave the US a commercial advantage and in this period Federal prosecutions of violations of obscenity law dropped from 32 in 1993 to 6 in 1997. The significance of US domination of the industry might justify it being seen as a form of American neo-colonialism as the industry was injected into both modern and traditional societies all over the world. Organized crime was heavily involved in the creation of the industry and in its day to day organization because of the amount of money to be made and the fact that it is a form of prostitution, which has always provided a happy hunting ground for crime groups.

Organized crime goes mainstream

Since the majority of the pornography industry has always been under the control of organized crime, the normalization of the industry can be seen as mainstreaming organized crime. The iconic 1970s pornography films *Deep Throat*, *Behind the Green Door* and *The Devil in Miss Jones*, which are credited with making pornography respectable for mainstream audiences, were directed by Gerard Damiano, who was involved with the mafia (Poulin, 2005, p. 121). Richard Poulin documents some of the history of mafia involvement. In 1975–80 there was a mafia war for control of the developing sex industry which led to 25 deaths in New York State alone. Poulin quotes the view of William Kelly, FBI investigator of the pornography industry, that it was impossible to be in the industry and not deal in some fashion with the mafia. He quotes Daryl Gates, chief of police in LA, who states that the mafia took control of the sex industry in California in 1969 because of the large profits to be made. In 1975 they controlled 80 per cent, whilst in 2005 they controlled 85–90 per cent.

Poulin details the origins of the Playboy empire in mafia control. When the Playboy Club first opened in 1960 in Chicago it was very much in the hands of organized crime. The alcohol licence was gained from politicians under mafia control, and the Chicago mob supplied the manager, waste disposal, parking, liquor and meat (ibid.). The Chicago mafia were heavily involved with strip clubs and pornography in Las Vegas too. In California in 2002 most of the production and distribution of pornography videos was in the hands of Joseph Abinanti, associate of the Lucchese crime family of New York (ibid., p. 123). The Philadelphia motor-bike club the Pagans is implicated in the sale of pornography in the US and biker gangs are involved in the industry in Canada too. Other organized crime groups internationally are involved in the pornography industry. Thus the Japanese Yakuza finances the pornography industry of the Netherlands (ibid.).

One good example of the way in which pornography mainstreams criminal activity is the reporting of, and attendance at, the funeral of James Mitchell and his brother, Artie, who were pioneers of the strip club and porn industries in the US. They opened the O'Farrell Theater in San Francisco in 1969 and had problems with police over the 'live sex shows and X-rated films they produced at the adult movie theater' (Coetsee, 2007). James served a prison sentence for 'fatally shooting the younger brother' he 'adored' (ibid.). James, like Larry Flynt, who set up the Hustler pornography and strip club empire now being franchised worldwide, and had a mainstream Hollywood film made vaunting his importance to the political freedom of Americans, *The People Versus Larry Flynt* (1996), is held up as an inspiration. Thus at his funeral San Francisco political consultant Jack Davis said: 'We all owe [our] personal freedoms to the brothers for the fights they fought on our behalf' and credited Mitchell for his part in transforming the adult entertainment from a 'dark, dank back room' business to a legitimate industry. Jeff Armstrong, the manager of the theatre, said: 'He was our Hector and our Achilles, and we drafted behind him.'

This mafia controlled business gained respectability in the late 20th century. Mainstream corporations got over any squeamishness they might have had as they saw the profits that could be made from distributing pornography. As the founder and director of Digital Playground said: 'I look at the porn business where Vegas and gambling was in the 70s. Vegas was still mob-owned and they were making the transition between these small groups of people to being corporate-owned. I feel the same exact thing is going to happen with adult' (Barrett, 2007).

The mainstreaming of pornography

The pornography industry is fast gaining so much legitimacy that mainstream finance houses are prepared to invest in it. The *New York Times* reports that the involvement of mainstream investors is 'in its infancy' (Richtel, 2007). 'Venture capitalist and private equity funds', it reports, are starting to show interest in pornography production and distribution companies. Thus the boutique investment bank Ackrell Capital has a 'growing practice' of 'matching investors with makers and distributors of sex-themed content'. Investors are attracted by 'public relations cover' from repackaging the companies in a 'more conventional way' so that they get a large part of their revenue from pornography but branch out into more mainstream areas as a cover. Thus Waat Media distributes content to mobile phones and has deals with several makers of explicit pornography, like Penthouse and Vivid Entertainment. In September Spark Capital, a mainstream venture capital firm, led a $12.5 million round of financing for Waat, but changed the company's name to Twistbox Entertainment and packaged the company as a 'mobile content distributor' (ibid.).

Pornography is now so mainstream that it forms a very lucrative sector of the business of respectable mainstream companies such as General Motors, which sells more pornography films annually than the Hustler chain (Poulin, 2005). General Motors previously owned DirecTV, a pornography distributor, which is now owned by Rupert Murdoch. The integration of mainstream media with the pornography industry helps to explain the way that pornography and strip clubs are normalized in the media. The Bank of Ireland has invested in Remnant Media, which is a porn producer. It can now be costly for mainstream companies to decide not to be involved with pornography. America Online, Microsoft and MSN have refused to allow adult businesses to set up shop on their services and do not accept ads from pornographers. But, Frederick Lane points out, when Infoseek was bought by Disney and made the same decision about pornography it was set to lose 10 per cent of its ad revenues, which are 95 per cent of overall revenues (Lane, 2001, p. 189). Credit card companies are implicated in the pornography industry because they are the main form of payment. The pornography companies nurture relationships with the card companies because they can be seen as high risk on the grounds of 'chargebacks', meaning situations in which customers refuse to pay a charge, perhaps because of the huge amount they find they have spent or because their female partner questions the statement. The pornography industry is careful to reassure bashful customers that the charges on their cards will be registered in such a way that they will appear innocuous to their wives. Thus AdultShop.com in Australia explains that purchases will 'be billed in Australian dollars and your statement will report your purchase as "AXIS Hume Au"' (see http://shop.adultshop.com.au/).

Adult Video News, the online magazine of the US pornography industry, claims that pornography videos are worth more than the legitimate Hollywood film industry and often use the same personnel. The industry is centred in Hollywood and creates more employment for Hollywood's army of film technicians and set personnel than mainstream production. It uses similar methods and language. Pornography production companies, for instance, now have 'contract girls' who are under contract to work for the company as film actresses used to be in the regular industry. There are more and more crossovers between the regular and pornography genres. Mainstream movies are made about the industry enabling men to see stripping and sexual acts in their local movie cinema. The regular industry becomes more and more pornographized, showing ever more graphic sexual activity. Another aspect of the normalization that is taking place is the way the music industry is becoming intertwined with the pornography industry. Whole genres of pop music now join with the newly respectable industry, with pornography actors doing signings at Tower Records, for instance. They market to the same consumers, young men.

The pornography industry has made great advances in gaining influence over mainstream politics, too. One example of this is the success of Richard Desmond, the famous UK pornographer and publisher of such top shelf titles as *Big Ones* and *Horny Housewives* and a 'live' sex website. In February 2001 the British Labour government approved Desmond's takeover of the tabloid newspapers the *Daily Express* and the *Daily Star* with money made from pornography. Eight days later the British Labour Party banked a £100,000 donation towards election expenses (Maguire, 2002). At the time, Desmond's most profitable business interests were in pornographic television channels, which provided 75 per cent of his pre-tax profits (Fletcher, 2002). Despite some critical reaction to what looked like a decision to hand two major UK newspapers to a porn king in return for a donation, in May 2002 Desmond was invited for tea at Downing Street to meet with Tony Blair. It is hard to imagine this degree of social acceptance of pornography and the sex industry as completely reasonable sergeants in arms to the Labour Party in the 1970s when pornography still had a disreputable air about it. The profits of the pornography industry are now so large that it is able to command considerable political obedience.

Desmond tried unsuccessfully to acquire the *Telegraph*, the *Sunday Telegraph* and the *Spectator*. Interestingly, for a pornographer who should surely be 'transgressive' if pornography apologists are correct, he has only been interested in ownership of right-wing newspapers. As a result of donations to charity he has had lunch at Buckingham Palace and in 1992 the Duke of Edinburgh officially opened the new headquarters of the company that runs his pornography magazines (Jones, 2000). He is now estimated to be worth £1.9 billion. He had plans afoot in 2007 to complete a £220,000 million floatation of Portland, his broadcasting business that includes pornography channels such as Fantasy TV and Red Hot TV (Judge, 2007). As proof that it is hard to be in the pornography industry without involvement with organized crime, Philip Bailey, Desmond's top aide, was badly assaulted by mafia thugs as a message to his boss in New York in the early 1990s. He had electric shocks administered to his genitals, had his face slashed with a box-cutter and was pistol-whipped in association with a conflict that Richard Martino, suspected of involvement with the Gambino family, had with Desmond over advertisements for dial-a-porn in Desmond's magazines. Martino and cohorts went on trial in 2005 over accusations that threats of mob violence were used to help them earn hundreds of millions of dollars in dial-a-porn and Internet pornography schemes (Robbins, 2005).

Production of pornography

Despite the determination of the defenders of pornography to claim that it is speech and fantasy, live girls and women do have their orifices penetrated to produce pornography. They take drugs to survive the pain and humiliation, and they bleed. Pornography has the harmful physical effects on women's health of other forms of prostitution, which include abraded vaginas and anuses, and considerable pain (see Holden, 2005). They include the physical harms of sexually transmitted diseases, unwanted pregnancies, abortions, infertility, diseases of the reproductive tract, that lead to complications in later life, and psychological harms (Farley, 2003). Many pornography movies are routinely made without condoms despite several pornography actors having been found, in the 1990s, to be HIV positive and to have passed on HIV on set to others. Harms can include infections of the eyes from 'money shots' when men ejaculate onto women's faces (Dines and Jensen, 2007). The girls subjected to these harms are most frequently very young, just 18 or younger, and extremely vulnerable, often homeless and with troubled family backgrounds from which they can draw no support, and with no money to live on (Lords, 2003; Canyon, 2004).

Those whose fortunes are created out of the sexual exploitation of girls and women in pornography can be quite frank about the harms involved. Thus Rob Stallone, who runs Starworld Modeling, a pornography pimping business in the US, comments: 'An 18–20 year old girl, is her life ruined if she does this? Ninety per cent of them, yeah. They make their $1000 a day, then they're out of the business and they don't have 20 cents' (quoted in Hopkins, 2007). He explained that at first the money seemed marvellous to young and vulnerable girls who had never had any: 'Young unknowns can come in, earn a grand for six hours of work, then do it all over again the next day. With $30,000 rolling in each month, they've soon got nice clothes and a flashy car' (ibid.). However, he acknowledged, many turned to drugs, and they found it hard to get other work when they were used up in pornography and no longer sought out. They could not show prospective employers résumés that only showed work in pornography and no qualifications. A difficult paradox exists for young would-be porn stars. To get work they have to perform more hardcore acts, and while that pays better, it also lessens their appeal for future work and tends to shorten their careers. The actress signs away rights to her image for US$1,200 whilst the really serious money will be made by those who sell and distribute it, since what started out as one scene can then be repackaged in endless compilation films or posted in perpetuity on the web. A pornography actress interviewed about working in the industry complained about the lack of preparation for the sort of work involved: 'In adult, there's no training. In any other business with some kind of risk, there's training. If you're working down on the docks in Long Beach, there's safety classes. There's nothing in this industry like that' (ibid.).

There is a burgeoning number of porn star biographies available, which give some information about the conditions the women experience, even though they seem to be written for pornography consumers and are rarely critical of the industry. In one such biography the European ex porn star Raffaela Anderson gives a useful description of what porn production entails for the young women who are abused in the process:

> Take an inexperienced girl, who does not speak the language, far from home, sleeping in a hotel or on the set. Made to undergo a double penetration, a fist in her vagina plus a fist in her anus, sometimes at the same time, a hand up her arse, sometimes two. You get a girl in tears, who pisses blood because of lesions, and she craps herself too because no one explained to her that she needed to have an enema … After the scene which the girls have no right to interrupt they have two hours rest.
> (quoted in Poulin, 2005, p. 138; my translation)

In recognition of such serious harms, Richard Poulin calls pornography the 'aestheticisation of sexual violence'.

Porn star biographies suggest that the girls who get involved have been made vulnerable by histories of sexual violence. Thus the famous porn star Traci Lords, who reveals in her autobiography that she began her brief career in pornography at 15 years old, was raped at the age of 10 by a 16-year-old boy (Lords, 2003). She was then subjected to sexual molestation by her mother's boyfriend. She became pregnant by a 17-year-old boy just after her 15th birthday and left home to seek money for an abortion, shelter and help from her mother's now ex-boyfriend. She lived with him and he pimped her into pornography, driving her to sets and taking the money. She was swiftly inducted into cocaine use, which was rife on the production sets. At first she posed for stills photography with her pimp masturbating with excitement at the side of the set. She was hired for use in *Playboy* while still 15. By 16 she was living with an abusive addict who pimped her and pressured her into hardcore 'live' pornography since she would otherwise get no work, and she earned $20,000 for 20 movies. One of them featured a group of women, including herself, being beaten and pretending to be ponies for a Japanese production company. She started stripping at the O'Farrell Theater at 16.

Another porn star, Christy Canyon, entered the industry at 18 and had to sign paperwork which asked her if she would do 'anal' or 'gang bangs' and whether there was any part of her body she did not want to be ejaculated upon (Canyon, 2004). She said she only wanted to do magazines, meaning stills. Three days later she was sent onto the set of a hardcore pornography movie by the pimping agency that hired her. She describes the pimp as being like a father figure to her and the only emotional or financial support she had. In these porn star biographies the common story is that the girls are young teenagers desperate for money, routinely homeless and with little self-worth or sources of emotional support. They are swiftly pressured into hardcore movies which they initially reject. If they do not accept, then the money dries up and they are on the street once more.

The cruelty of the practices they are thus forced to engage in, as well as the hatred of women that the pornography films represent, is revealed in the descriptions on the Adult Video News website of the movies it reviews. The description of the production of a 2005 title in AVN shows the cruelty involved as the woman being prostituted here endures lengthy anal penetration by two penises.

> Cock-crazed Audrey is lighting up the room to critical mass levels with her blinding, nuclear-strength energy, taking multiple man hammers ... two and three at a time, in her mouth, cunt and ass for the better part of a very sweaty hour.
>
> 'Goddamn! Fill me up like a fucking fuck whore!' she roars to one and all, the depraved blast furnace heat making her heavy makeup run down her pretty face all Alice Cooper-like. Audrey even sets a supposed new porn record (such records being

dubious at best) for length of time doing continuous double anals – 18 minutes (breaking, she tells me, Melissa Lauren's old 17-minute mark).

The scene is shot by the dynamic duo of Jim Powers and Skeeter Kerkove, the latter of whom just oozes pure joy at the porn-making process. 'Look at that double anal!' he exclaims excitedly at one point, full of kid-in-a-candy-store glee. 'This is better than a holiday in Cambodia.'

(Adult Video News, 2005)

Cambodia is mentioned because, as we shall see in the next section, the desperation of the women and children for subsistence has made it into a haven for western sex tourists and pornography production companies.

The globalization of the pornography industry

The pornography industry is now international in its production and distribution, in the trafficking in women which it facilitates, and in the damaging effects it has on women's status in non-western cultures in which pornography is a new harmful practice. As the industry expands it seeks both new and cheaper environments in which to produce the materials and new markets into which to sell it. Elements of the pornography industry choose to make porn movies in countries in which women are vulnerable to severe forms of exploitation and can be paid a pittance. One good example of what could be seen as the outsourcing of risk (Haines, 2005) is an American company producing sadomasochist materials for the website 'Rape Camp' using cheap and compliant Vietnamese women in Cambodia where the excitement for male consumers in seeing them raped was enhanced by racism (Hughes, 2000). The particularly severe sexual exploitation of women in Cambodia is a result of the way in which the sex industry was developed to serve the militaries that took part in the wars in the Mekong sub-region before 1975, particularly US soldiers. As Donna Hughes explains, this Phnom Penh resident announced in 1999 that he was adding a live bondage sex show to his Internet site which features 'Asian sex slaves' used for 'bondage, discipline and humiliation' (ibid.). The women were 'blindfolded, gagged, and/or bound with ropes while being used in sex acts; some had clothespins clipped to their breasts'.

Viewers were, Hughes reports, encouraged to 'humiliate these Asian sex slaves to your heart's content'. There was to be pay-per-view access in which customers could request torture to be carried out in real time at up to US$75 for 60 minutes. The website also offered prostitution tourism to Cambodia. The pornographer, Don Sandler, used Vietnamese rather than Cambodian women as he thought this would create less local outrage.

He was outsourcing women's subordination as well as risk, as he made clear in answering suggestions that the website might provoke violence against Cambodian women. He said he expected the market to be in America and he was happy for women to be attacked there: 'I hate those bitches. They're out of line and that's one of the reasons I want to do this ... I'm going through a divorce right now ... I hate American women.' The Cambodian Minister of Women's Affairs stated that this constituted violence against women and Sandler was arrested. United States officials ensured that he was not prosecuted but deported back to the US. Donna Hughes identifies this incident as one example of the expansion of the global sex industry that has resulted from '[t]olerance and *de jure* and *de facto* legalization of prostitution and pornography', which have 'increased men's demand for women and girls to be used as sexual entertainment or acts of violence'. Sandler's activities in Cambodia marked the beginning of a big expansion in live sex shows via the Internet through companies such as Private Media Group operating by satellite out of Barcelona (Hughes, 2000). In 1999 this company broadcast simultaneously to 1,000 customers.

It is not just adult women that are being exploited in the production of pornography in Cambodia. UNICEF has decried the use of Cambodian children in pornography. Cambodian media have pointed out that children as young as seven are freely available from video disk vendors in Phnom Penh, and the films have Khmer language titles such as *Luring Underage Child* and *70-year-old Grandfather Rapes 9-year-old Girl* and include scenes of bondage and sexual abuse (*Cambodia Daily*, 2007). The impact of the global pornography industry in Cambodia extends beyond the harm it creates for women and children used in its production. Research suggests that the availability of pornography to children in Cambodia is having a profound effect on attitudes to sexuality and on sexual practice. One study was conducted in response to several assault cases by minors on minors in which the perpetrators claimed they had been influenced by pornography (Child Welfare Group, 2003).

The researchers interviewed 677 minors in Phnom Penh and three provinces. They found that 61.7 per cent of boys and 38.5 per cent of girls had viewed pornography. Pornography was openly on display and sold at news-stands, coffee houses, video shops, underground businesses and by market vendors. Some coffee shops show pornography throughout the day and the customers are all male. The coffee has to be paid for but the pornography is simply an enticement.

Some of the effects of watching pornography on young males were indicated in group interviews. In one interview group, for instance, the boys said that they 'enjoyed watching violence, and that most men do' (ibid., p. 17). When they were asked how it made them feel, one boy replied: 'We want to do what we see.' The boys said they did not hurt women but would 'use strong language and raise their voices to prostitutes after watching these films' (ibid., p. 17). However, they also said that they were sure that watching violent pornography made men violent towards women and encouraged rape and that they believed that women enjoyed being hit during sex because it heightened the women's sexual pleasure. The authors say that though their evidence is anecdotal is suggests there may be a 'desensitizing effect' from pornography. They comment that it is clear that minors use pornography as a means to obtain information about sex. The boys explained that they went to watch the films at coffee shops every evening as they had nothing else to do, and that if they could afford it they would visit a prostitute afterwards. They added that 'it is not possible to watch these films without having sex or masturbating afterwards, and that it isn't uncommon for men who cannot afford a prostitute to pick up a girl off the street and rape her' (ibid.).

Pornography may have even more profound effects in traditional communities, where it has been identified as playing a part in normalizing sexual abuse and prostitution for children and young people. Where pornography is introduced quite suddenly to an indigenous culture it may be possible to identify more easily the ways in which women's status is damaged. In western societies pornography has been normalized over 40 years. As this has taken place the rhetoric of sexual freedom, free speech and sexual liberation has been used to justify it. It may be hard now for citizens to turn around and observe the harm that pornography has wrought because its values have become so much a part of many areas of culture (Jeffreys, 2005). In traditional communities, however, pornography can be seen as having a similarly dramatic effect to that of the Christian church, which was brought to Pacific societies by colonizers in the 20th century. Christianity undermined traditional sexual practices through categorizing as unchristian sexual activity which did not take place in Christian marriages. The impact of pornography has been arguably equally powerful in promoting a new sexual value system, but in a very different form. This new form of cultural colonization is largely about spreading the value system of US pornography, since the US is the main fount of the pornography that penetrates these societies. As Stiki Lole comments in an article on changing sexual practices in the Solomon Islands: 'While Malaitan Kastom and Christianity are still influential, young people's sexual practices are influenced also through globalizing processes, including the increased movement of people and exposure to radio, television and videos, pornography and the Internet'(Lole, 2003, p. 219).

Pornography has been pinpointed as a significant factor in the transformation of sexual practices and attitudes in traditional Australian aboriginal communities where there has been, in recent decades, an epidemic of child sexual abuse and violence against women. In 2007 the *Little Children Are Sacred* report (Wilde and Anderson, 2007) gained much media coverage for its disturbing revelations about child sexual abuse in communities in the Northern Territory. It supports the importance of pornography in creating this devastation. The report states that the issue of children's and the community's response to pornography was 'raised regularly' in the communities that were visited (ibid., p. 199). The authors comment that 'use of pornography as a way to encourage or prepare children for sex ("grooming") has featured heavily in recent prominent cases'. They say that in written submissions community groups and individuals expressed concern at the way in which children were exposed to pornography. This exposure was attributed to poor supervision, overcrowding and the normalization of the material. The report is clear that the effects are harmful, stating that '[t]he daily diet of sexually explicit material has had a major impact, presenting young and adolescent Aboriginals with a view of mainstream sexual practice and behaviour which is jaundiced. It encourages them to act out the fantasies they see on screen or in magazines'.

The report also blames pornography for the advent of sexualized behaviour evident in young people and even in young children who act out sexually and aggressively towards each other. Some examples of the sexual abuse that were occurring in the communities included an 18-year-old boy anally raping and drowning a six-year-old girl who was swimming with friends at a waterhole, an 18-year-old boy digitally penetrating the vagina of his seven-month-old niece, and a 17-year-old boy who would regularly show pornographic DVDs at a certain house and then get young children to act out the scenes from the films. The report states that there is 'increasing sexually aggressive behaviour by both boys and girls' and teenagers are becoming 'more violent, more sexual and more anarchic' (ibid., p. 66). There was a high rate of sexually transmitted infections (STIs) and of pregnancy in children aged 12–16, and increasing 'consensual' sex between children. The problem had got to the point where in one community 'girls did not understand that they had a choice to refuse sex. They accepted that if they walked around at night they were available for sex' (ibid.). Many, if not all, of these children had either been sexually abused themselves, had witnessed inappropriate sexual behaviour through pornography, or seen others having sex in front of them. The pornography was seen in the communities as having broken down the traditional cultural constraints which would once have made such behaviour unthinkable. Pornography is available in the communities through pay-TV via Austar as well as through DVDs. Austar says that there is blocking software available to block the pornography it distributes, but instructions for this are only available in English, not aboriginal languages. One group interviewed for the report identified the state TV channel whose brief is the showing of multicultural programmes, SBS, as another source of pornographic programmes, which it mainly shows on Friday evenings. Another group complained about both pornography videos and music videos with pornographic content, as well as regular TV and magazines with pornographic content, and another commented that 'it was often white fellas who would come in and sell the pornographic DVDs' (ibid., p. 199).

Shamima Ali's UNICEF study of violence against the girl child in five Pacific nations also points to the infiltration of pornography into these traditional societies and the role it plays in the creation of prostitution industries and the sexual exploitation of girls (Ali, 2006). She explains that men in Papua New Guinea (PNG) are 'spending the family's cash income (derived from royalty payments or from their wife's small business) on pornography and prostitution, thereby fuelling industries which demean women and girls' (ibid., p. 7). The spread of pornography, she says, and 'its easy accessibility in many Pacific countries' is believed to 'significantly increase the risks to the girl child of becoming a victim of sexual violence' (ibid., p. 7). In countries where resource exploitation is taking place, such as Papua New Guinea and the Solomon Islands, she points out, there is internal labour migration among males to mines and logging camps where they live away from their families. This fuels markets for video pornography as well as prostitution and leads to the sexual exploitation of girl children. In Fiji the main forms of sexual exploitation include pornography as well as prostitution, sex tourism and adoption.

In Carol Jenkins' fascinating study of the changing sexual culture of PNG one interviewee describes the change in behaviour that pornography has created. She says that in her youth she slept with boys but they were only allowed to rub noses. This had changed because '[o]ur minds are now full of sex. We see white people naked and kissing on the TV screen and books' (Jenkins, 2006, p. 10). Jenkins reports that '[m]edia, especially video and pornographic magazines, also play a large part in the changing ways of sex' (ibid., p. 30). In focus group discussions in her study, pornography was held responsible for 'increased rape, heightened sex drive, and the spread of STIs' (ibid.). The comments of one of her informants strikingly depict the way that pornography can affect a boy who has not been brought up with the expectations of a western pornographic culture. He was asked what movie he last saw and responded that he could not remember but 'it was acted by white people ... I saw them naked, they played around with their sexual organs, sucking each others' sexual organs – they f*** like wild dogs' (ibid., p. 30). He said he could not 'control my feelings. I lost control, my penis expanded and expanded. Some of the boys, when they saw it, they held on to their expanded penis and tried to control it, but they couldn't ... when I came outside, when I saw girls I really was tempted to rape them. I wanted to put into practice what I saw that made me sexy' (ibid., p. 30).

The changes in sexual culture have led to extremely high rates of gang rape in particular. Jenkins comments that group rape is culturally specific to PNG, where it accounts for at least half of all rapes and is referred to locally as 'lineup, deep line, single file and plural copulation'. Of the youth in this study, 11 per cent of women and 31 per cent of men reported personal involvement in lineups. Where men were concerned this was mostly on numerous occasions, and 40 per cent of men also admitted raping women when alone. In a national rural study 61 per cent of men said they had participated in group sex at least once, and 65 per cent of women said they had been raped, often with the use of weapons. Sexual violence, she considered, was so common as to be seen as normative in many communities.

Conclusion

The pornography industry stimulates the expansion of many other areas of the global sex industry and creates the male clients who use the strip clubs and brothels. Its profitability tempts major corporations to become involved and it is attracting the interest of banks and investors. The practices and products are evolving very fast and show considerable variety, from phone sex to live sex websites. But as the industry expands internationally it draws in girls and women around the world whose bodies are the sites in which the profits are made. Women in poor South East Asian communities can now go into a booth in an Internet café and create live pornography for customers in other countries who instruct them on what to do (personal communication with Coalition Against Trafficking in Women member from the Philippines). Men can sell the sexual use of their wives and children internationally online. As the production and distribution of pornography are globalized it is transforming sexual cultures all over the world, with harm to the status of women and girls. In the 1990s the strip club industry, sometimes called 'live pornography', was normalized too, as we will see in Chapter 4, and it has had similarly worrying effects upon the women and girls who are exploited within the industry and the status of women.

The strip club boom

There has been a rapid expansion of the strip club industry in the western world in the last decade, particularly in the form of lap dancing clubs. The industry is estimated to be worth US$75 billion worldwide (D. Montgomery, 2005). Some writers in the field of gender studies have defended the practice of stripping. They have argued that stripping should be understood as socially transgressive, an exercise of women's agency or a form of empowerment for women (Hanna, 1998; Schweitzer, 1999; Liepe-Levinson, 2002). These arguments exemplify the decontextualized individualism which is common to many defences of the sex industry. However, the tradition of women dancing to sexually excite men (usually followed by commercial sexual use of the women) is a historical practice of many cultures, as in the case of the auletrides of classical Greece, who were slaves (Murray and Wilson, 2004), and the dancing girls of Lahore, who are prostituted within their families from adolescence (Saeed, 2001). It does not signify women's equality. Rather, the tradition of stripping signifies sexual inequality and it is most prevalent, historically, in societies in which women were very much second class citizens. This chapter will examine the context in which stripping takes place, looking at who owns the industry and who benefits most from it, in order to expose the weakness of the argument that stripping is a form of women's empowerment. It will look at the evidence that suggests that both national and international organized crime gangs run the most profitable sectors of the industry. It will show how, as the industry both expands and becomes more exploitative to create greater profits, the trafficking of women and girls into debt bondage has become a staple way of sourcing strippers in Europe and North America. Rather than empowering women, this chapter will suggest, the strip club boom helps to compensate men for lost privileges.

The strip club boom

Striptease is not a new phenomenon in the west. However, in the 20th century the practice was gradually decensored and became increasingly explicit in the amount of nudity and touching permitted: from *tableaux vivants* in which women were not permitted to move and had to wear skin-coloured coverings, to the lap dancing of the present. In the latter, women are usually naked and use their genitals to massage the penises of clothed men whilst seated on their laps in private booths. Customers for the recent expansion of the industry are likely to have been trained and encouraged in the commercial sexual use of women by the decensorship of the pornography industry from the 1960s onwards. Many of the clubs and chains set up in the boom are owned by men who got rich through pornography, such as the Hustler chain of Larry Flynt.

In the 1980s striptease moved into a new phase. Prior to this time it was traditional for clubs to pay women to dance. The change began in the United States. Dawn Passar, a former stripper who now organizes the Exotic Dancers' Alliance, explains that when she first danced in San Francisco the well-known venue the Mitchell Brothers' O'Farrell Theater, whose operations were mentioned in Chapter 3, 'paid wages, minimum per hour and tips' (Brooks, n.d.). The Market Street Cinema in the same city introduced 'stage fees' in which dancers had to pay management for the right to dance, making a living through tips from private dances, and this spread to the other venues. This was a profound change which enabled the venue owners to make much more considerable profits. They were now charging the dancers instead of paying them. From this point on the amount of the 'stage fee' rose very fast, to the point where women sometimes dance with no profit for themselves in an evening, or even make a loss. This new level of profitability and the new principle that workers should pay to work, stimulated the strip club boom. The US industry was estimated in one media report in 2006 to be worth much more than baseball: '$4 billion a year is spent by men on baseball, the national pastime. Compare that to $15 billion a year spent by men at strip clubs' (Sawyer and Weir, 2006).

The feminist debate

In response to this boom in strip clubs it might be expected that there would be a lively feminist discussion of the issue, but this is not so. Feminist critiques of stripping are thin on the ground. Instead there are many articles and books which represent stripping as an exemplification of Judith Butler's ideas of the transgressing of gender through the performance of femininity and masculinity (Butler, 1990). Liepe-Levinson, for instance, in a book in the Routledge series 'Gender in Performance', argues that strip shows involve 'social transgressiveness' because female dancers 'play desired sex-object roles as they openly defy the expectations of the double standard' (Liepe-Levinson, 2002, p. 4). Dahlia Schweitzer, in the *Journal of Popular Culture*, also argues that stripping is transgressive (Schweitzer, 1999). Striptease, in her view, enables women to role reverse and take power over men: 'With men the suckers, and women pocketing the cash, the striptease becomes a reversal of society's conventional male/female roles. Striptease is, at its core, a form of role removal' in which women are 'clearly in charge' (ibid., p. 71). She gives the impression that a pro-stripping line is the correct feminist position when she argues: 'By removing her clothes, the stripper disrupts years of patriarchal hegemony' (ibid., p. 72). The anthropologist Lynne Hanna, on the other hand, takes the approach of pure American liberal individualism (Hanna, 1998). She both researches and writes in the field of dance studies and now serves as an expert witness on behalf of the strip club industry in cases where local authorities seek to exercise control over strip clubs. She argues that attempts to limit strip clubs and activities in the US violate First Amendment rights to freedom of communication. Her conclusion is that '[i]t is time to cease stripping the First Amendment, corseting the exotic dancer and patron, and tying up the community and to promote equality of opportunity for everyone' (ibid., p. 21).

This form of literature on strip clubs, much of it written by women who have experience in the industry, tends to stress the agency that women who strip are able to exercise. Katherine Frank, who worked as a stripper before researching a PhD on strip clubs and their patrons, says that she had 'increased feelings' of 'self-efficacy' when 'dancing', though she acknowledges in her work that the fact that she was known to be a graduate student and had other options is likely to have made her personal experience untypical (Frank, 2002a).

She is critical of the notion that stripping is transgressive. She seeks to create a 'feminist politics of stripping' and writes of how she 'performs' femininity through the practice, but argues that the male buyers are not aware of the 'performance' and 'hold very normative views about gender roles'. She is forced to ask whether the transgression works: 'What is the effect of my double-agent approach to womanhood on the men who gaze up at me? The hard truth is that I cannot predict or prescribe how my performances will be interpreted' (Frank, 2002b, p. 200). Frank is well aware that there are constraints on the exercise of agency. She speaks, for example, of stripping being 'deeply intertwined with gendered and sexual positionings and power relations' (Frank, 2002a, p. 4). But she is quite positive about what stripping offers to women. Frank speaks, for instance, of the 'potential economic and personal rewards' and the 'radical political potential of mixing money, sexuality, and the public sphere' so that 'sex work cannot be dismissed as a possible form of feminist resistance or an exercise in female agency' (Frank, 2002a, p. 16). Of strippers she writes: 'We open spaces of resistance within the heteronormative culture of the strip club and elsewhere' (Frank, 2002b, p. 206). The constraints themselves, such as the structural dimensions of the industry, the exploitative and abusive practices of strip club owners, managers and clients, restrictions on how much money is made by women who strip and what precisely they have to do to get it, are scarcely mentioned.

Though there is now a considerable feminist literature on the harms of prostitution, looking at the effects on prostituted women psychologically and physically (Farley, 2004; Jeffreys, 1997), this has not been the case for stripping, where there is little analysis of the harms. Feminist research has only just begun to address the effects of this boom on other women, such as those in the neighbourhoods where the clubs are set up, and those who seek equality in a business world where, in some sectors, the majority of deals take place in strip clubs from which they are excluded (Morgan and Martin, 2006). A literature is just beginning to develop on the gains that the male buyers make from their involvement in the strip club industry. Most significantly there has been a conspicuous gap in the literature in relation to the context in which the stripping takes place. The feminist literature does not discuss who is developing this industry and who benefits. This chapter begins with an examination, mainly from media reports, of the context of stripping, looking at who owns the industry, the involvement of organized crime and the trafficking of women that supplies it. The second part looks at the harms suffered by the women who strip within this exploitative context using the little research which exists combined with material from strip club industry magazines and sex work organizations. The third part looks at the impact of strip clubs on equality between the sexes through the experience of the male buyers, and that of the women in the world of business who have to confront a new glass ceiling created by male colleagues' use of strip clubs, using some interesting recent research in this area.

The context of the strip club industry

Strippers do not work independently. The practice takes place in clubs which are extremely exploitative. The clubs are often part of national and international chains which, according to the work of investigative journalists in the UK and the US, have criminal connections (Blackhurst and Gatton, 2002). This context is likely to affect the potential for empowerment. The strip club industry is expanding because of the profit levels in the business. In the US in 2005, there were an estimated 3,000 clubs, employing 300,000 women (Stossel, 2005). In 2002, there were 200 lap dancing clubs in the UK (Jones *et al.*, 2003). A 2003 media report estimated the annual turnover of UK lap dancing clubs at £300 million and commented that 'they are one of the fastest growing elements in the UK's leisure services industry' (ibid., p. 215). The strip club industry is estimated to be worth £22.1 million a year to the Scottish economy alone (Currie, 2006).

Spearmint Rhino, the American chain owned by John Gray, now has clubs in the UK, Moscow, Australia, as well as the US. British investigative journalists Jonathan Prynn and Adrian Gatton report that the Tottenham Court Road, London, club makes profits of more than £3 per minute (Prynn and Gatton, 2003). In 2001, a year after it opened, the club made a 'tax profit of more than £1.75 million from sales of £7.8 million, equivalent to takings of £150,000 a week' (ibid.). Over the Christmas period the revenues were £300,000 a week. They point out that a busy city pub would take only around £20,000 pounds in a good week and this goes a long way to explaining why many pubs in the UK have been converted to strip clubs in recent years. Spearmint Rhino operates in the common style of lap dancing clubs, with dancers paying £80 per night to work and the club taking 35 per cent of the earnings from customers.

Media reports suggest that some strip club owners and managers are associated with organized crime. This is relevant to the degree of 'empowerment' that is likely to be available to strippers. The owners of strip clubs are careful to represent themselves as upstanding members of the community in their sponsorship of football teams, donations to charity and so on. The owners of upmarket clubs promote them as elegant destinations for socially élite men. However, there are indications, despite all attempts to maintain the veneer of respectability, that strip club owners have disreputable associations. One indication is the amount of unexplained death and injury sustained by the owners/managers and their associates. The manager of Spearmint Rhino UK, a supposedly upmarket chain, was viciously attacked whilst walking from the Tottenham Court Road club to the car park in 2002 (Blackhurst and Gatton, 2002). 'Two men came up behind, struck him on the head with a machete and knocked Mr Cadwell to the ground. He somehow fought back but was stabbed at least twice, one blow puncturing a lung' (ibid.). No one was charged and the police 'suspect this was no ordinary street robbery, that Mr Cadwell was targeted by associates of a notorious north London crime family in a feud with his company' (ibid.). An unexplained death occurred in relation to Cadwell when, in September 1990, a 21-year-old woman who was riding with him in his helicopter in California was killed. She was the girlfriend of Cadwell's close friend David Amos: 'She stepped out of the helicopter as it stood on the tarmac at Long Beach Airport to greet Mr Amos, who was waiting for her, and walked into the still turning tail rotor blades.' The police investigation concluded the death was an accident. In 2001 Amos was convicted of the machine-gun killing of a strip club boss in Los Angeles in 1989. He was close to a member of the Bonnano mafia family in New York and had paid a hitman to shoot Horace McKenna at his home (ibid.). An attack similar to that on Cadwell took place in Edinburgh in 2005. The manager of one of Scotland's biggest lap dancing bars 'was stabbed as he locked up for the night' (J. Hamilton, 2005). The *Sunday Mail* reporter notes: 'Police believe he may have been caught up in a feud between the capital's gangsters' (ibid.).

John Gray's Spearmint Rhino is the most successful international chain. These clubs go to particular lengths to establish that they are upmarket venues and not just 'strip joints' and are popular with business executives for entertaining clients. Gray, however, is a controversial figure. He has six convictions in the US for offences ranging from carrying a concealed weapon to writing dud cheques, for which, collectively, he received a suspended sentence, 68 months probation and periods in jail (Blackhurst and Gatton, 2002). According to an *Evening Standard* (London) investigation, though 'born John Leldon Gray … he has used the names, John Luciano, John Luciano Gianni and Johnny Win' (ibid.). The *Standard* article makes the interesting point that '[o]ddly, there is also a John L Gray, born in February 1957 and linked to two Spearmint Rhino addresses and one of Mr Gray's home addresses, who is registered in the US as "deceased"' (ibid.). Journalists in different countries are clearly interested in the connections between organized crime and the strip club industry but have to be careful what they say in case of libel claims.

Arguments about women gaining agency and empowerment through stripping need to be looked at in the context of the extent of organized crime involvement in the industry. Organized crime employers and managers are men who bully, threaten and kill to gain their profits. This needs to be factored in as a powerful form of inequality between the sex entrepreneurs and those they exploit. It is interesting to note that one of the arguments made for legalizing the prostitution industry in many countries where brothels are still illegal is that this will drive out organized crime, which only thrives because the illegal industry is driven underground. But strip clubs are legal everywhere and persons connected with organized crime are running them and collecting the considerable profits.

An approach of decontextualized individualism is inappropriate for analysis of stripping because, unlike the women who strip, the club owners and entrepreneurs are very organized nationally and internationally. They are not operating simply as individuals. Many are involved in networks of organized crime. But even those for whom there is no evidence of such involvement are organizing together to influence, and in many cases bribe, politicians, to engage lawyers and experts who can swap ways to avoid regulation and defeat community activism. These networks are organized through associations and online resources such as the US newsletter of the Association of Club Executives, *Strip Magazine* in Europe and the Eros Foundation in Australia.

As a result of their careful efforts to achieve respectability, such as sex exhibitions, stripping competitions, support for charities and a positive coverage in the media, strip clubs have experienced a remarkable normalization. Such leading figures of the UK establishment as Margaret Thatcher, Prince Harry and Tony Blair's son Euan have all been recorded as patronizing the clubs in 2005/2006. Thatcher was a guest at a Tory Party fundraiser in Peter Stringfellow's London club in April 2005 (Strip Magazine, 2005). Euan Blair was observed 'spending the evening in the Hustler club late in November while on work experience in Paris' in 2005 (Strip Magazine, 2006). In April 2006 Prince Harry was observed at a lap dancing club: 'He [Harry] and a group of mates arrived at Spearmint Rhino at Colnbrook near Slough, Berks, at 3am … Harry grabbed a seat near the topless dancers – and stripper Mariella Butkute sat on his lap' (Rousewell, 2006). Meanwhile the industry is promoted in the business pages of newspapers, in how-to books and, currently, in some academic disciplines such as business studies (Jones *et al.*, 2003) and leisure studies, where it is described positively in a leisure studies collection as 'a satisfying leisure experience' and 'passive recreation' (Suren and Stiefvater, 1998).

Trafficking

Despite the attempts of the strip club entrepreneurs to promote themselves and their venues as respectable, trafficking in women by organized crime groups has become a common form of supply of dancers. All over Europe and North America women and girls are brought into the clubs by deception, by force or, initially, by consent. In all cases they are kept in debt bondage, have their travel documents confiscated and are controlled by threats to themselves or their families, all the traditional aspects of this modern form of slavery. Governments can be complicit in the trafficking of women to strip clubs, acting as procurers for the business. In Canada, for instance, the importation of women was organized through exotic dancer visas issued by the state. Visas for particular skilled occupations which could not be staffed by local employees were a formal part of the immigration programme; 400–500 visas a year for Eastern European women were issued until 2004. In order to gain visas women had to supply proof that they were strippers, and this was accomplished by the provision of 'soft-porn' pictures to immigration authorities (Agence France-Presse, 2004). Audrey Macklin argues in *The International Migration Review* that local strippers could not be found because the conditions of work in stripping had deteriorated drastically with the advent of lap dancing and private booths (Macklin, 2003). Canadian citizens were not prepared to experience the extreme degradation involved. Macklin makes the fascinating argument that the strippers from Eastern Europe should be seen as the 'spoils of war'. She explains: 'If the fall of the Berlin Wall symbolizes the defeat of communism and the triumph of capitalism, then perhaps commodified East European women, exported to serve Western men, are the spoils of the Cold War served up by the global market to the victors' (Macklin, 2003). The soldiers of liberty from the west, in the form of strip club habitués in North America and Western Europe, can claim and use the bodies of women of the defeated communist régime. They exercise the colonizing power of rich males within a globalized economy.

The strip club owners have such power and influence within national economies that they are able to get governments to act as procurers for their industry. Macklin explains that Mendel Green, lawyer for the clubs, asserted that the state owed a duty to the private sector to provide labour inputs where market incentives failed (Macklin, 2003). Indeed he is quoted in a newspaper at the time as calling strippers 'products', saying: 'They're a critical sort of product in the entertainment industry that is not readily available in Canada' (*Guelph Mercury*, 2004). Interestingly, Green argued that foreign women were needed because 'Canadian-born dancers were controlled by biker gangs' (ibid.), which is an admission by an industry representative of the involvement of organized crime. The Canadian government became sufficiently embarrassed at so clearly acting as a pimp to the local strip club owners that the exotic dancer visas were discontinued in 2004.

Trafficking of women from Eastern Europe into strip clubs has caused considerable concern in Ireland. Until 2002 the Irish state, like Canada, issued work permits for lap dancers under the category of 'entertainment', thus making the trafficking effortless (Haughey, 2003). Justice Minister Michael McDowell told the parliament in 2002 that 'there was clear evidence that human traffickers from Eastern Europe used lap dancing clubs as a front for the sex trade' (Wheeler, 2003). In June 2003 the Gardai in Ireland 'blocked a bid by Eastern European organized crime gangs to take control of the money-spinning lap dancing industry' (Brady, 2003). The gangsters were thought to have links with paramilitaries and criminals in Ireland. The *Irish Times* comments that the industry is 'plagued' by reports that prostitution occurs in the clubs and in Dublin one club was closed by a court order after illegal sex acts were found to have been taking place (Haughey, 2003). The feminist anti-violence organization Ruhama argues that the clubs 'groom' women for prostitution and 'in every other country in the world they are just a cover for prostitution' (ibid.). There is trafficking into the clubs in the US too. In an example from 2005, 'a Russian entertainment promoter Lev Trakhenberg of Brooklyn, NY got 5 years for admitting he and his wife helped more than 25 women to come illegally from Russia to the United States to perform nude lap dances at strip clubs' (Parry, 2006).

Exploitation and violence towards strippers

It is in the context of huge profits to club owners, of organized crime and trafficking, that women strip in the clubs. The profits would not be so large if women were being fairly remunerated for stripping. In fact the vast majority of the profits go to the club owners, and not to the dancers, who may find it hard to earn enough to pay the stage fees. In San Diego dancers 'can make several hundred dollars on a weekend night, but most struggle to make $100 a night, many of them earning only what they can make in tips ... Another dancer at Minx Showgirls ... said she averages closer to $45 a night' (Washburn and Davies, 2004). The strip club habitué of 25 years, Tyke, who writes for the industry journal *Strip Magazine* explains that the idea that UK dancers can make £2,000 a night is a myth. It is in fact a story frequently repeated by club owners, who would find it hard to attract dancers if they told the truth. Tyke explains that 'to make £2,000 in 1 night would involve 100 table dances i.e. around 15 an hour for a typical 7 hour shift, I just don't think that happens' (Tyke, 2004). He explains that 'girls' might in exceptional circumstances find a merchant banker who will spend his 'Christmas bonus' and that could create the much touted large earnings.

The profit levels in the industry are enhanced by the fact that strippers do not get the benefits that other club workers receive, such as sick leave or superannuation, since the club owners treat them as individual agents who simply rent space in the club. As Kelly Holsopple points out in her research on stripping, although the club owners argue that they are not employers and that the strippers are independent agents, they control hours and schedules, fees and tips and even set the price of table dances and private dances (Holsopple, 1998).

They pressure dancers to engage in complete shaving of pubic hair, year-long tans or breast implants. They regulate when women can use the bathroom, when they can mix with other women and when they can smoke. The rules are enforced with fines for being late, for calling in sick, for 'talking back' to customers or staff and many other infringements which can deplete their earnings. Many of the offences for which the strippers are fined are in fact invented. On top of this strippers have to tip those who are employed by the club on regular wages. Managers enforced 'a mandatory tip out to bouncers and disc jockeys' (ibid., p. 3). Liepe-Levinson also writes of fines for minor transgressions, and harsh work schedules (Liepe-Levinson, 2002).

As the clubs seek to maximize profits they put on greater numbers of dancers, which creates greater competition, forces down earnings and pressures strippers to engage in violating practices they would rather avoid such as lap dancing or prostitution. 'Retired' stripper Amber Cooke explained in a 1980s collection on sex work that strippers are forced, because there are too many dancers and not enough male buyers, to compete and 'encourage hands-on enter- tainment rather than dance, in order to make their money' (Cooke, 1987, p. 98). She points out that this is 'dangerous' and bouncers are not an effective protection because they cannot watch all tables, let alone the more recent private booths, and may be 'reluctant' to back up a stripper against a group of aggressive male customers. The advent of lap dancing in strip clubs has been seen by stripper advocacy groups and individual dancers as creating severe harms. When carried out in private booths it enables male buyers to sex- ually assault women, and to engage in forms of intimate contact that the women find intolerable. In a Melbourne court case a man was jailed in July 2006 for raping a stripper in a private booth: 'During the dance, she took off her G'string and was naked. Her breasts were about 30cm from Nguyen's face ... [he] lunged at the woman, digitally raping her ... he pinned the woman to a couch' (*The Australian*, 2006).

Canadian strippers formed an organization to oppose the develop- ment of lap dancing in the clubs, and those interviewed in one study particularly objected to having to come into contact with 'customers' ejaculate', which could occur 'when ejaculate penetrated the men's clothing during lap dances' (Lewis, 2000, p. 210). One interviewee explained: 'So halfway through the song, like no warning, you're sitting on their lap, and all of a sudden you're wet.' Another concern was 'dancers' genital contact with other dancers' vaginal secretions, left on customers' clothing'. These lap dancing opponents also talked of the harm they experienced from being pressured by owners and managers and customers to engage in lap dancing, and being threatened with job loss if they did not comply. Such practices made them feel 'disempowered and victimized'. Two dancers said that they were crying their eyes out' after their first night of lap dancing, and were distressed by '[t]hese strangers' fingers all over you – it was really nasty' (ibid.). Nonetheless, the researcher, Jacqueline Lewis, opposed the ban on lap dancing that many of her interviewees saw as necessary for their survival in the industry. She considered that the solution to the problems strippers faced was to treat stripping just like other forms of work. But there are no other forms of work apart from the sex industry in which women have to battle to keep men's fingers and ejaculate off their naked bodies.

There has been very little research on the physical and psychological harms that strippers face in clubs. Indeed, information on the harms of stripping may be hard to elicit for some researchers. Thus Danielle Egan, who writes about stripping from what she calls a 'sex radical' perspective and rejects radical feminist analyses which focus on harm, comments that the women she worked with as a stripper and interviewed for her book avoided elaborating on their 'experiences with bad nights' (Egan, 2006, p. 83). Egan interpreted bad nights as those on which women got very little money and were made to feel bad or 'like whores' and the good nights as those on which they made money and felt good. She does not enlarge on the women's experiences of being touched by men or having to touch them and how they felt about such practices. This more detailed analysis is hard to come by. Kelly Holsopple, who worked as a stripper in the US for 13 years, conducted research into the harm of the industry to the dancers (Holsopple, 1998). She argues that the 'common underlying element in strip clubs is that male customers, managers, staff, and owners use diverse methods of harassment, manipulation, exploitation, and abuse to control female strippers' (ibid., p. 1). Holsopple conducted 41 interviews and 18 face to face surveys followed by discussions.

Her interviewees did not report the empowerment of women or expression of agency that some gender studies scholars have attributed to stripping (e.g. Egan, 2006). Women had to engage in activities they did not want because their income was 'entirely dependent on compliance with customer demands in order to earn tips'

(Holsopple, 1998, p. 3). Holsopple concludes from her interviews that in abuse by the male buyers 'customers spit on women, spray beer, and flick cigarettes at them' and they are 'pelted with ice, coins, trash, condoms, room keys, pornography, and golf balls' (ibid., p. 8). Missiles included a live guinea pig and a dead squirrel. Women were hit by cans and bottles thrown from the audience, and male buyers also 'pull women's hair, yank them by the arm or ankle, rip their costumes, and try to pull their costumes off'. Women are commonly 'bitten, licked, slapped, punched, and pinched' (ibid.). The male buyers attempt to penetrate women vaginally and anally with 'fingers, dollar bills, and bottles'. Successful vaginal and anal penetration was common.

Holsopple's study showed that women suffered particular harms from the conditions in which they were required to dance. They had to dance on elevated runways so narrow that they could not get away from men on either side touching them. In the context of private dances men openly masturbated and 'stick their fingers inside women'. Wall dancing, for example, 'requires a stripper to carry alcohol swabs to wash the customer's fingers before he inserts them into her vagina. His back is stationary against the wall and she is pressed against him with one leg lifted' (Holsopple, 1998, p. 6). Holsopple's interviewees described clearly the forms of pressure and sexual harassment that they experienced from the male buyers in private dances: 'I don't want him to touch me, but I am afraid he will say something violent if I tell him no' and 'I could only think about how bad these guys smell and try to hold my breath' or 'I spent the dance hyper vigilant to avoiding their hands, mouths, and crotches' (ibid.). All of the 18 women in her survey reported being both physically and sexually abused in the clubs, and receiving verbal harassment, often multiple times. Most had been stalked by someone associated with the club, from one to seven times each. Holsopple says that regulations that customers should not touch dancers are 'consistently violated' and 'stripping usually involves prostitution' (ibid.). Liepe-Levinson reports that the strippers she interviewed experienced pressure to provide sexual favours to bosses and employees (Liepe-Levinson, 2002).

The advice offered to strippers from within the industry or from state funded sex work agencies on how to avoid violence supports Holsopple's findings of the dangers associated with stripping. On the *Strip Magazine* website, for instance, Ram Mani offers advice on how to be constantly alert to all the possibilities of men's violence (Mani, 2004). Women are advised not to leave the clubs alone. Outside the club they should get straight into their cars and lock the doors, moving off immediately. They should not take a direct route home and should keep an eye on the mirror to check they are not being followed. They should park neither too far from the club so they have a dangerous walk to get to it, nor so close that a man may be able to take the registration number. When they register their cars they should do so to another address than their home one. They are warned: 'The odds of being stalked, mugged and attached [*sic*] are on increase and you must always keep your guard up' (ibid.). The advice offered to strippers by the sex work advocacy website STAR in Toronto includes tips for combating sexual assault: 'Watch for roaming hands. Clients have an easier time touching you when you dance on a box, specially when you're bending over' (STAR, 2004). Dancers are told to '[w]atch out for unruly or aggressive customers' and to '[u]se the mirrors to keep track of your back'. There is specific advice for private dances since 'there's a greater possibility of assault', which is: 'If a customer is trying to manhandle you, try holding his hands in a sexy way to control him. But be aware the touching violates some municipal bylaws. If you're being assaulted, scream' (ibid.). The strip club industry is thus dangerous and abusive for the women involved in it, but the harms of this industry stretch beyond the clubs themselves to affect the status and experience of other women.

Reinforcing gender inequality: the glass ceiling for women in business

Women in a society in which strip clubs flourish are likely to be affected by them in a variety of ways. Women whose husbands, partners, sons, male friends and male workmates visit strip clubs will suffer some effects. Wives and partners of pornophiles, for instance, report in interviews that they suffer harms such as losing self-esteem as men compare them with the women in pornography, having to do poses and practices that come from pornography to satisfy their male partners, and losing needed family income to men's obsession with pornography (Paul, 2005). Frank's research found that men reported visiting strip clubs to get revenge on their wives if they had an argument, and were well aware of the distress that their behaviour would cause if wives knew of it, and did cause to wives who suspected (Frank, 2002a). When areas of cities are commandeered for men's sexual commodification of women, women who are not in the sex industry are likely to feel excluded from these spaces. Whilst men may take for granted their right of being able to access public space freely, women have always suffered a reduction in this right because of male violence and its threat.

Strip clubs are not separate from society but affect the way men relate to women on many levels. One area of harm in which legal cases are now being brought and research is just beginning to be done relates to the obstacles strip clubs place in the way of equality for women in the business world. A fascinating 2006 study (Morgan and Martin, 2006) shows how women professionals are blocked from engaging in the vital social networking which secures clients and contracts. It explains that many women professionals 'traverse other settings beyond the office in the course of their work', including conferences, aeroplanes, hotel rooms and lobbies, restaurants, shop floors, golf courses, tennis courts, sporting events, bars, cars and trade shows (Morgan and Martin, 2006, p. 109). The study explains that '[e]mployer-sponsored out-of-the-office socializing with colleagues, customers and suppliers is institutionalized'. In this way day-to-day work is done as well as the 'relationship building' that 'embeds the foundation for reciprocity and long-lasting organizational ties in personal ones' (ibid.). Thus this out-of-office socializing has important purposes which are completely necessary to a woman's work and career, not optional at all. The authors of the study, Morgan and Martin, explain that entertaining clients at strip clubs is an ordinary part of the work of the sales representatives they were researching in many industries. They write: 'Accounts from industry trade magazines suggest that almost half of salesmen, but only 5 per cent of saleswomen, had entertained clients in topless bars' (Morgan and Martin, 2006, p. 116). Saleswomen, they point out, are excluded from 'industry contacts and denied access to professional information exchange'. The interview information they were examining showed that some of the women professionals were disgusted by the visits to strip clubs, whilst others were just angry that they were excluded by being sent to their hotel rooms whilst the men went on to the clubs. The entertainment receipts showed the clubs as restaurants so that the accountants did not have to know where the events took place.

There is plenty of evidence to suggest that when men enter strip clubs in groups the atmosphere is even more exaggeratedly masculine (Frank, 2003; Erickson and Tewksbury, 2000).

As Morgan and Martin put it: 'Patrons tend to be louder and more raucous. The male-bonding bravado permeates the entire audience to some degree. The level of objectification of the dancers also appears to increase as a result of this phenomenon' (Morgan and Martin, 2006, p. 118). Women are not able to join in this bonding, which is expressly constructed between men through their objectification of naked women. Saleswomen said that at such events 'they undermined the "cavorting" and "fun" and ultimately the "bonding" that the events were intended to promote' (ibid.). One woman described trying to attend a strip club with a customer and two company managers. She ended up speaking, and perhaps bonding, with the strippers rather than her male companions, saying: 'And I'm like, "Okay where do I look?" I'm talking to the strippers' (ibid.). Her interaction with the strippers would be likely to humanize them and provide an impediment to the men's enjoyment of objectification.

The practice of taking clients to strip clubs seems to be particularly common in the finance industry. An estimated 80 per cent of city workers (presumably male ones) visit clubs such as Spearmint Rhino in London as a part of their work. This came out in a court case about the poaching of clients between two London finance firms in 2006 (Lynn, 2006). The journalist reporting on this interesting piece of information comments helpfully: 'In effect, just as their fathers might have taken clients to one of the gentlemen's clubs of Pall Mall, so brokers today take their business associates to see lap dancers. The old gentlemen's clubs banned women – some still do – whereas the lap-dancing establishments merely intimidate them' (ibid.). He explains that if one bank won't let its workers take clients to lap dancing clubs then its rivals certainly will. In the US this form of exclusion of women from equal opportunities has resulted in some high-profile actions for sex discrimination against top finance houses by women employees. Morgan Stanley, for instance, in 2004, agreed to pay $54 million to settle Equal Employment Opportunity Commission (EEOC) charges that it had 'discriminated against women in pay and promotions, and tolerated crude comments about sex and men-only outings to strip clubs with clients' (Lublin, 2006). The woman who sued said in the lawsuit that she was left out of a client entertainment weekend in Las Vegas because 'the men would be uncomfortable participating in sexually oriented entertainment with a woman colleague present, especially one who knew their wives' (Summers, 2007). Another company,

UBS, paid out US$29 million to a former director of international equities who had a number of complaints which included being invited by her manager to a 'bottomless' club (ibid.).

The practice of men in business fraternizing in strip clubs extends to politicians on the business of the state too. In 2007 it was revealed that the leader of the opposition Labour Party in Australia, Kevin Rudd, a committed Christian who is now Prime Minister, visited the strip club Scores in New York while on official business observing the UN (Summers, 2007). He was invited by Col Allen, editor of the *New York Post*, owned by Rupert Murdoch, to go to the club along with Australian Labour MP Warren Snowdon. Anne Summers, Australian journalist and director in the 1980s of the Equal Opportunities Commission, writes of her disappointment that this visit was greeted with jovial acceptance in the Australian media despite being a practice that discriminates against women. She points out that the practice of business and political entertaining in strip clubs can be very big business in terms of the amount of money spent. Scores strip club, she points out, 'settled a contested bill of $US241,000 charged to the American Express card of the former CEO of information technology company Savvis' (ibid.). The newspaper in the Kevin Rudd story is likely to have picked up the bill. The use of strip clubs for discriminatory male bonding activities offers opportunities for corruption too to men in business and political élites as they hobnob with another male network, organized crime. The Scores club was controlled in the 1990s by the Gambino mafia family (Raab, 1998).

So integral and accepted have the strip clubs become within corporate culture that their importance to business is now being used as an argument as to why town councils should encourage their development (Valler, 2005). When the issue of granting a lap dancing club licence was before the council in Coventry, UK, in 2005, a 'leading businessman' argued that 'a lap-dancing club would boost Coventry's reputation as a major centre of commerce ... When businessmen travel to a major city where they stay overnight, they almost expect to find a lap-dancing club. If Coventry has aspirations to be a major business area, then it has to have a quality adult entertainment area, and that would include a lap-dancing club' (ibid.). Strip clubs are an aspect of the international sex industry which is integral at present to the way that men do business, politics and crime, albeit through the bodies of naked women. The effect is to reinforce the glass ceiling for those women in business and the professions who are permitted to keep their clothes on in male company.

Reinforcing gender inequality: a masculinizing practice

Concomitant with the losses women experience from the existence of strip clubs, there appears to be a direct enhancement of men's self-esteem, their feelings of masculinity and their bonding with other men. Though there is little evidence from research on strip club practices to suggest that the strippers experience a reversal of gender roles, and an access of power, there is, however, some very interesting research on what the male buyers gain in terms of personal power in relation to women from visiting the clubs. Katherine Frank used her status as a stripper to gain access to male customers and interview them. Her work is most revealing on the motivations of buyers (Frank, 2003). She studied men in traditional strip clubs that did not provide lap dancing, and reports that none of the men she interviewed said they went to the clubs for 'sexual release'. They had other motives, of which the most common were the 'desire to relax' and visiting a place where they could 'be a man' (Frank, 2003, p. 6). Frank explains that the clubs 'provide an environment where men, singularly or in groups can engage in traditionally "masculine" activities and forms of consumption frowned upon in other spheres, such as drinking, smoking cigars, and ... being "rowdy", "vulgar" or aggressive' (ibid.). Strip clubs recreate the gendered spaces for men that were challenged in second wave feminism. In the 1970s and 1980s some major campaigns were directed at stripping away from men the privilege of having male-only spaces in which to socialize and do business where women were not allowed. These campaigns included demanding and achieving women's entry to public houses, to sporting clubs and other places of entertainment on an equal basis with men. The boom in strip clubs can be seen as a counterattack, in which men have reasserted their right to network for and through male dominance without the irritating presence of women, unless those women are naked and servicing their pleasures.

Frank found that an important reason for men to visit the clubs was that they provided a compensation for the decline in power that they experienced as their wives, partners and women workmates shed their subordination, began to compete with them and demanded equality. The strip clubs provided an antidote to the erosion of male dominance by institutionalizing the traditional hierarchy of gender relations. The men found everyday relationships with women 'a source of pressure and expectations' and described relations between women and men in general as being 'strained', as 'confused', or 'tense'. One buyer referred to the 'war between the sexes'. They sought respite from the problems of having to treat women as equals in the workplace too. One of Frank's respondents, Philip, said that he was able to 'let frustration out', particularly about 'this sexual harassment stuff going around these days, men need somewhere to go where they can say and act like they want'. Some buyers, Frank found, 'desire to interact with women who were not "feminist," and who still want ... to interact with men in "more traditional" ways'. One of these traditional ways, it seems, is women's unconditional servicing of male sexual demands. Other buyers told her that, outside the sex industry, 'men had to continually "be on guard" against offending women'. Franks points out that 'several of the above comments could be analysed as part of a backlash against feminism' but says that she prefers to see them as a result of confusion caused by feminism and women's movement towards equality, as falling within 'a framework of confusion and frustration rather than one of privilege or domination'. She does say, however, that the rapid increase in strip clubs in the US in the 1980s 'was concurrent with a massive increase of women into the workforce and an upsurge of attention to issues of sexual harassment, date rape' (ibid.). 'Many' of the men she spoke with said they were confused about what women expected of them in relationships, and particularly when wives worked, had their own incomes and wanted to be included in decision making.

Frank considers that what takes place in the clubs does more than compensate men for these changes. The visits to strip clubs can be understood as 'masculinizing practices' in their own right. In the clubs otherwise unattainable women could be subjected to the men's control, exercised through the ability to refuse payment, over the length of their conversations with the women, what would be discussed and whether and when the women had to strip. Men reported that they got an 'ego boost' because there was no fear of rejection or of competition with other men. Frank concludes that strip clubs help to reinforce male power, through maintaining 'imbalance in the power dynamics in personal relationships with women, especially when they are used to shame or anger wives or partners' (ibid., p. 74). However, she remains determined not to place too strong an emphasis on this. She remarks, despite the evidence she presents, that '[t]his is not to say that commodified sexual exchanges are inherently about the preservation and reproduction of male power' (ibid., p. 75).

Another study of strip club patrons by two male researchers supports Frank's findings about the role the clubs play in upholding male dominance (Erickson and Tewksbury, 2000). The study analyses how the 'ultra-masculine context of the setting affects and illuminates patrons' motives for frequenting strip clubs' (ibid., p. 272). This study also points out that the men in the clubs are in control as the women are bound to 'reciprocate most of the attention paid to them by the customer' rather than being able to reject male attention as they can in the world outside (ibid., p. 273). The customer 'may dictate the nature, and often the course, of the interactions because the dancer is both obligated and financially motivated to cooperate with the direction of the customer in defining the interactions' (ibid.). This study confirms Frank's argument that the clubs are male-only environments that confirm masculinity, 'it is almost exclusively a "man thing" to go to strip clubs. It is one of the very few places where men have the opportunity to openly exhibit their latent sexual desires and to perform their "male privilege"' (ibid., p. 289). The 'context' of the strip club serves to affirm masculinity because it is 'pervaded by images and norms that openly objectify women, is ultra-masculine' (ibid.). They conclude, however, in a way which seems to contradict their earlier findings, by saying that their study contradicts the notion that strippers are exploited because the dancers 'control the sequencing and content of their interactions with patrons and, in doing so, they generate a substantial income for themselves and provide men with access to important social commodities' (ibid., p. 292). In their view, this is a fair exchange. Yet earlier they explicitly state that the men are in charge of the interactions, because the women cannot reject their advances as they can in the world outside the clubs, and they provide no evidence of the good earnings of the dancers. Their research thus seems to represent a male buyers' perspective.

Unlike the traditional gentlemen's clubs of London's Pall Mall, the strip clubs offer the opportunity to debase women, not just to bond and do business in their absence. The new gentlemen's clubs require women to be present, but only when naked and available to be bought. Men can drink with their friends whilst staring into a woman's genitals or shoving their fingers into her anus or vagina. The context in which the male buyers are delivered this bounty is created for them by masculine networks of owners and franchisees.

Conclusion

The strip club boom needs to be fitted into understandings of the industrialization and globalization of the sex industry. An examination of the context of the strip club boom, of the way that profits are made, of the involvement of organized crime, of the trafficking of women and girls into the clubs, of the violence and exploitation that takes place, makes the arguments of some liberal feminists that dancers are empowered by stripping, able to exercise agency and transgress gender relations, look very thin. Such arguments represent a decontextualized individualism which takes no account of existing inequality between men and women and the way that strip clubs can only derive from and serve to reinforce this. Rather, I suggest, the strip club boom represents a rebalancing of the power relations of male dominance, away from what has been gained through feminist movements and the social and economic changes of the last quarter-century. It does this through its role in international capitalism and organized crime, the masculinizing effects of club patronage on male buyers, the subordination of hundreds of thousands of women in the clubs, and the exclusion of women from equal opportunities in national and international professional and business networks of men who use the clubs to bond and do business. The strip club boom imports into the west degrading practices developed in the poor countries of South East Asia to service the US military in rest and recreation. The norms of military prostitution were globalized. Women danced and waited to be chosen, in the west for 'lap dances', ostensibly, and in South East Asia for other forms of prostitution, as we shall see in Chapter 5.

Chapter 5

Military prostitution

Military prostitution was a most important vector in the globalization and industrialization of prostitution in the late 20th century. The massive industrialized militaries of the 20th century understood that prostitution was necessary to their military preparedness. The male soldiers were provided with easy, organized, cheap and 'safe' access to prostituted women. The prostituted women were recruited in a variety of ways. The 'comfort women' were kidnapped, deceived or bought from parents in Korea, China and other invaded and colonized countries for the Japanese military brothels of the 1930s and 1940s. The women and girls used by peacekeepers in brothels in Kosovo are trafficked women kept in debt bondage, mostly from Eastern Europe. The methods are strikingly similar but the degree of official involvement by militaries and state governments varies. Military prostitution on a scale similar to that employed by the Japanese was part of the US military rest and recreation régimes after World War II throughout South East Asia. This formed the basis for the huge sex industries and trafficking of women that developed in Korea, Thailand and the Philippines, and became such important sectors of their economies. In its sheer scale, military prostitution can be seen as kickstarting a crucial aspect of the globalization of prostitution, the sexual exploitation of a sexual proletariat of women and children from poor countries by members of rich westernized nations.

Feminist concern with military prostitution dates back at least to the UK campaign against the Contagious Diseases Acts (CD Acts) of the 1860s and the subsequent international campaign against state regulated prostitution (Jeffreys, 1985a, 1987). The CD Acts were introduced, ostensibly, to protect servicemen from venereal diseases and the temptation of homosexuality. The Acts decreed that women in designated areas near camps and ports who were suspected of prostitution could be arrested, examined and locked up in 'lock' hospitals if found to be infected. Feminist outrage at that time, from the iconic anti-prostitution feminist Josephine Butler and others, was at the violation of women's rights in this regulation of provision by the state of women for men's use. This system of state regulation started from military prostitution and presages precisely how military prostitution was organized in the 20th century in Asia for Japanese and then American troops – the women were compulsorily inspected and registered whilst the men were not. The CD Acts campaign was successful, with the Acts being suspended in 1886. Unfortunately their equivalent exists today in legalized prostitution systems in Australia, for instance, in which women prostituted in brothels have to be examined and the prostitutors do not (M. Sullivan, 2007).

The problem of sexual exploitation by militaries was raised early in second wave feminism. Susan Brownmiller showed how militaries used rape to punish vanquished male populations by stealing 'their' women, and to gee up their soldiery to battle-ready aggression (Brownmiller, 1975). In the 1980s Cynthia Enloe made military prostitution an important issue for international feminist theory in her work on militarization (Enloe, 1983, 2000). Enloe explained that the problem for analysis was not so much militaries as militarization, or the gearing of societies for conflict in ways which profoundly affected their economies and everyday politics. The creation and maintenance of huge, war-ready militaries requires the involvement of hundreds of thousands of civilians, and particularly women, to bolster and service them. Many of these women are those inducted into prostitution. The masculinity of troops is, in this feminist understanding, deliberately created by militaries through the provision of prostitution and pornography, which enable men to 'other' women.

The othering of women is fundamental to basic training, in which men are accused of being women in order to toughen them up. Without the concept of 'women' as social inferiors from whom the male soldiers must differentiate themselves by their actions, the male soldier might have no founding myth to hang onto, no rationale (A. Carter, 1996). When US soldiers buy prostituted women for use in rest and recreation in areas which have often been supervised by military police, as in Korea, they are further working to differentiate themselves from women and to develop the aggressive masculinity which will enable them to kill others (Moon, 1997; Sturdevant and Stoltzfus, 1992). They affirm male bonding by visiting brothels in groups. Women soldiers are deprived of this bonding activity and, presumably, of the other benefits that the US military considers that prostitution provides to its male soldiers. They are not equal in this respect but represent precisely in their persons the 'others' on and in whose bodies the male soldiers are being trained to be men. Some feminist critics of the military and of militarization have pointed out not just that the military is a masculine institution, as are other institutions that women seek to enter such as the police force or fire service, but that it requires masculinity in order to function (Jeffreys, 2007; Enloe, 2000; Morgan, 1989).

The use of prostitution in its many forms to comfort and entertain soldiers, to pump them up, to maintain their military aggression, is pervasive across militaries and conflict zones. Pornography can be used in military training too, to encourage soldiers to distinguish themselves from women and develop their aggressive masculinity. Pornography was used, for instance, to encourage aggression when the Pakistani army invaded Bangladesh in 1971. Brownmiller reports that '[i]n some of the camps, pornographic movies were shown to the soldiers, "in an obvious attempt to work the men up," one Indian writer reported' (Brownmiller, 1975, p. 82). Hundreds of thousands of rapes of Bangladeshi women were carried out by the soldiers who had been so thoroughly 'worked up'. Ruth Seifert makes the important point that militaries make offers of masculinity to soldiers. Male soldiers expect a consolidation of their masculine status and receive this from training and the male bonding around violence in warfare. Ruth Seifert calls this 'the elevation of masculinity that accompanies war in western cultures' (Seifert, 1994, p. 65).

Though they are generally critical of military prostitution, there is some disagreement amongst feminist commentators over the extent to which particularly severe forms of sexual exploitation should or could be separated out from the ordinary run of military prostitution. The feminist literature tends to rank the different forms in which militaries organize their troops' sexual access to women according to perceived degrees of harm. Thus the form which creates the most outrage and condemnation is what is commonly referred to as 'sexual slavery'. 'Sexual slavery' is separated out by some scholars from prostitution, and depicted as distinct because women were obviously kidnapped, forced or deceived, or did not get paid, or because of the severity with which the women were treated, such as being killed after a period of sexual use in Bosnian camps. Ustinia Dolgopol, for instance, argues that the abuse of the 'comfort women' should not be seen as prostitution, but rape (Dolgopol, 1996). The Japanese government, in its consistent and continuing representation of the comfort women system as voluntary prostitution which was not organized by the state, and thus does not require that the survivors be compensated, has pushed activists into the argument that it should be seen as military sexual slavery or rape (Lys, 2007). In this chapter I will seek to show the continuities, rather than the discontinuities, between the different forms of military prostitution.

Military sexual slavery

The comfort women system

Yuki Tanaka takes the approach of looking for continuities, saying that in its essence the 'comfort women' system was not much different from other forms of prostitution or sexual violence against women (Tanaka, 2002, p. 181). He explains that it emerged from the state organized brothel prostitution systems of Japan, and of Korea under Japanese rule, where about 200,000 of the victims, the vast majority, originated. It did, though, he considers, resemble most closely the rape camps of Bosnia-Herzegovina. The difference between the comfort women system and other forms of military prostitution lies in the degree of brutality, and in the fact that the Japanese system was organized from the highest echelons of the military, which planned and implemented it in cooperation with state authorities.

He explains the phenomenon as arising from the particular historical situation of Japan at that time. It was going through a swift change from feudalism to capitalism, skipping the stage of bourgeois revolution that would normally intervene. Thus the régime was still dominated by feudal and patriarchal ideologies. The first Japanese military brothels were set up exclusively for the military in Shanghai in 1932 as Japan's colonial expansion into Asia began to accelerate. Previously Japanese brothels were privately run and not just for troops. Women in the military brothels were examined twice weekly for venereal disease and the provision of brothels was expected to deter the rape of civilians, which had the unfortunate effect of alienating subject populations and creating 'anti-Japanese sentiment'. The 'comfort women' selected were mainly Japanese at first, drawn from the women and girls sold by their families into brothels. In some areas of China women were requisitioned by requiring local Chinese security councils to provide women for the purpose. By 1938 there was a full-scale mobilization of Korean women. Japanese pimps and procurers were employed too, being asked to come to China and set up private brothels stocked with Japanese women.

The fact that all this was planned and organized from the top levels of the military is plain. Senior staff officers issued orders to establish the brothels, which were put into operation by staff officers of units on the ground. Those involved were all élite army officers, some of whom were members of the Japanese government. The recruiting methods included using agents or labour brokers, who used the classic methods by which the trafficking in women still takes place in the present: 'deception, intimidation, violence and even kidnapping' (ibid., p. 21). Often the privilege of first sexual use of the virgin girls went to officers. The scheme, however, failed to control rape. In some areas of Korea, for instance, unofficial 'comfort stations' were set up, in which women were simply abducted, kept in military compounds and raped for months. This is very similar to what took place in Bosnia, and Tanaka suggests that prostituted women in this form of prostitution should be called 'sexual slavery hostages' rather than 'comfort women' (Tanaka, 2002, p. 47). The girls selected were young and virgins because they were considered to be less likely to be suffering from venereal disease. The requisitioning of women in the Philippines was slightly different. They were abducted from their homes or kidnapped when walking in the street by groups of soldiers. They were held captive for from one month to two years in army compounds rather than separate brothels. About 10 young women and girls were held by each unit for the use of its members. Girls from the Philippines and China were very young, even as young as 10 when 'requisitioned'. Some Filipino girls saw their family members killed before they were abducted.

The 'comfort women' system as it operated in Rabaul in Papua New Guinea shows clearly the degree of state responsibility. The historian Hank Nelson points out that this site is little known about despite the fact that when Australian troops re-entered the territory, which Australia administered before the Japanese invasion, after the war there was plenty of evidence and there were both Australian and local eye-witnesses to provide details (Nelson, 2007). Nelson, like other serious researchers, dismisses the notion that there was no official state involvement in the system and the idea that private entrepreneurs just set up brothels to service the troops on their own initiative. The women were observed being brought in on troop ships, and so swiftly after the original landing that it is clear that they were not travelling 'privately' but organized by the state. About 3,000 women were shipped to military brothels in Rabaul.

The brothels in Rabaul were euphemistically, and with great disrespect to the women who are thus officially designated as 'goods' to be stored, called 'special warehouses'. Australian witnesses said that the women came from Japan, China and Korea. The brothels were graded so that the Japanese women in kimonos were set aside for the use of officers, whilst the women from Japanese conquered territories used in other brothels were kept in worse conditions and looked down at heel. The fact that a small proportion of the 'comfort women' were Japanese has been used by some to suggest that the system was indeed one of the voluntary prostitution of women who were already prostituted and 'chose' to take this opportunity to make a better living. In fact the Japanese women were likely to have been enslaved in prostitution very young when sold by impoverished families, so that 'choice' on their part does not have much meaning. Moreover one witness described the Japanese women as 'little more than children'. The Korean women were deceived, told they were coming south for work in factories and on plantations and then imprisoned in the brothels. They had an average of 25–35 clients per day. Many perished when the Japanese were forced off the island and ships taking them out were bombed.

Descriptions of how the Japanese military brothels functioned show that they did not differ substantially from the way prostitution takes place currently in legalized or tolerated brothel systems. The girls were trafficked in after deception, or sale, suffered terrible violence if they resisted rape, were told that they were in debt and therefore indentured. This is very similar to what takes place today when trafficked women are placed in legal brothels in Australia (Fergus, 2005). The 'comfort women' suffered 10 men per day outside periods of combat, but before and after action they suffered 30–40 men per day. Men are described as shaking with anticipation in the long queues outside the brothels. The women in the comfort women system describe severe pain and the swelling and bleeding of their genitals. Descriptions of harm in the legalized brothel system in the state of Victoria in Australia have some commonalities with the pain and injury that 'comfort women' complain of. Kate Holden, for instance, explains that the first difference she noticed when she was sexually used in the brothels was a burning vagina since in street prostitution she had only had to do oral sex (Holden, 2005). In the Japanese system soldiers paid at the front desk and received tickets that they gave to the women, who were supposed to receive half the fee but in reality usually got extremely little or only tips. The fee system works much the same way in the brothels in the legalized system of Victoria, Australia (M. Sullivan, 2007), except that in Victoria the prostituted women would expect to receive one-half to two-thirds of what the prostitutors paid. In the Japanese system prostituted women were expected to clean their genitals with creosol after each use by a man but often had no time for this, and some used the creosol to commit suicide (Tanaka, 2002). Women in legalized brothel systems in the west today are unlikely to use such harmful chemicals on their genitals, but they do use douches, and local anaesthetic to dull the pain, as we shall see in Chapter 8. Those who advocate a sex work position in relation to brothel prostitution are unlikely to emphasize such similarities, but a consideration of the common experiences of women who are warehoused for men's sexual use in systems of state sanctioned or organized prostitution can be useful in demonstrating the common harms of prostitution.

Comfort women for the US postwar

The US military, which was to be the major force in constructing military prostitution in the post-World War II world, partook of the 'comfort women' system too. In the immediate postwar period the Japanese government was concerned that the US occupation troops would rape Japanese women if they were not supplied with prostituted women as a substitute. They thought this particularly because they were well aware of their own troops' propensity to rape. Thus they constructed as deliberate state policy a comfort women system for the US military. A memo from the Home Ministry's security division instructed police chiefs to 'aggressively lead and quickly establish sexual comforting institutions' (Lie, 1997, p. 257). The thousands of women required were to be recruited from women already in prostitution, 'geisha, licensed and unlicensed prostitutes, waitresses, barmaids, habitual prostitutes and the like' according to the official instruction to police chiefs (Tanaka, 2002, p. 134). The US and allied forces had already made plans, apparently, to set up military brothels as they advanced (ibid., p. 87). Not all the women were already in prostitution, as some high-school students working in munitions factories were recruited by the mafia groups closely linked with fascist political organizations, who acted as procurers. These students, who had lost their families in the war, were almost certainly deceived. They were gang-raped by groups of GIs as their induction. Some of the brothels were set up specifically to entertain high-ranking US officers and top delegates of the US government's missions. There were always 20 'top geisha' on hand to send to the dinner parties of high-ranking officers.

Some of the brothels set up at this time for the US military were so large that they can be seen as presaging the industrialization of prostitution. One had 300–400 women and was set up in the dormitories of an ex-munitions plant (Tanaka, 2002, p. 153). The total number of prostituted women being used by occupation troops in Tokyo alone at the end of 1945 was an estimated 10,000, with 70,000 overall (Lie, 1997). The state worked with private club and brothel owners to set up the Recreation and Amusement Association (RAA), which has been called 'the world's biggest white-slave traffic combine', with capital of 50 million yen, of which 35 million yen was provided by the Finance Ministry. The state recruited by advertising for 'special women employees' for 'comforting stationed troops' and some women signed up because there was massive hunger and unemployment (ibid.).

Genocidal sexual slavery: 'rape camps' in Bosnia

There are considerable similarities between the comfort women system and the rape camps set up by Serb militias in Bosnia. The signal difference between what was inflicted on Korean, Chinese and Filipino women by the Japanese military, when they were kidnapped or bought and imprisoned in brothels, is that this took place in a context of colonization and war but not 'genocide'. In Bosnia the experience of women and girls kidnapped for rape camps was regularly fatal. Since the 'ethnic cleansing' of a whole people was underway, murder was just an ordinary part of business (Stiglmayer, 1994). Once the women had outlived their usefulness or novelty value, there was no reason to keep them alive, except in those cases where women who had been impregnated were seen as useful in diluting the ethnic purity of the enemy, in which case pregnant women were deliberately sent back to their own side to cause humiliation. Catharine MacKinnon calls attention to the continuities between the rape camps and the pre-existing sex industry. She explains that the 'rape camps' were a product of attitudes towards women that already existed in Yugoslavia before the war when Yugoslavia was saturated with pornography. She quotes a Yugoslav critic of the system as saying that the pornography market in the former Yugoslavia was 'the freest in the world' (MacKinnon, 2006, p. 163). 'When pornography is this normal', she says, a whole group of men 'is primed to dehumanize women and to enjoy inflicting assault sexually' (ibid., p.164). One effect of the Serb combatants' familiarity with pornography was that they made pornography of their rapes of non-Serb women as propaganda, even seeking to change the ethnicity of those involved so that the violence could be seen as being perpetrated on Serb women to gee up their own side. Considerable misogyny was expressed: 'Sometimes those who were watching put out cigarette butts on the bodies of the women being raped' (ibid., p. 165). As we have seen earlier in this volume, this practice of burning women with cigarettes is one of the forms of violence women in strip clubs in the US have to suffer (Holsopple, 1998).

In another genocide, under the Nazi régime in Europe, a different version of 'rape camp' prostitution was instituted in concentration camps and in ghetto imprisonment, about which Catharine MacKinnon offers fascinating information and insights (MacKinnon, 2006). The Warsaw ghetto was ordered by the Nazi health department to set up a brothel of fifty Jewish women for the use of German soldiers, despite the fact that such fraternization was forbidden. Himmler required the creation of 'at least' nine brothels in concentration camps by the end of the war. Women in the camps were forced into the brothels to service particular categories of male prisoners or into army and SS brothels. The women in the brothels for foreign workers, MacKinnon explains, were the same nationalities as the slave labourers. Some volunteered in order to get enough to eat. Men who used the camp brothels in which Jewish women were incarcerated were mainly Jewish but included block seniors and Kapos. In some places Jewish women were imprisoned for use by the élite SS guards (ibid., p. 217). As MacKinnon puts it: 'In the Holocaust, a corrupted political economy of force targeted Jewish women for prostitution in all its forms, integrally to the genocidal destruction of the Jewish people' (ibid., p. 218). The prostitution of Jewish women was part and parcel of the other practices of extreme violence, from sexual assault to murder, that were carried out upon them, thus '[o]n admission to the camps, women were made to strip and stand genitally exposed on two stools where they were internally searched and genitally shaved while being sexually ridiculed' (ibid., p. 219). One SS officer, she explains, 'had the custom of standing at the doorway ... and feeling the private parts of the young women entering the gas bunker' (ibid., p. 219).

US military rest and recreation in South East Asia

US military prostitution is not usually included in 'military sexual slavery', though there are some clear similarities. The similarities include the sheer numbers of women mobilized to service the military, and their containment in large-scale brothel areas, the methods used to obtain women, the practices the women were compelled to experience, and the involvement of governments and military commands in setting up and overseeing the system. The difference would seem to be in the degree of violence involved, such as the fact that the comfort women system involved the deaths of very large numbers of the prostituted women, as did the Bosnian rape camps. In Korea the US military prostitution system built on the Japanese system, and was instituted just five years after the war. It followed the licensed brothel system already set up in Korea by the Japanese in the 1920s, which provided a template for the comfort women system. US military prostitution was the foundation of the sex tourism industries of the Asian countries in which it was set up, and therefore a very important motor force in the industrialization and globalization of prostitution. Though the direction and organization of the US government is not quite so clear as in the comfort women system, US military prostitution was created out of the cooperation of the militaries with the governments of countries in which the troops were based or which they visited for 'rest and recreation', R&R.

Katharine Moon (1997) explains that the military prostitution industry in Korea was established during the Korean War (1950–3). Before the war there was prostitution of 'camp followers' by the US military but it was informal and unregulated. It took place in the

US barracks and in makeshift dwellings. There was no R&R system offering 'a myriad of sexual fantasies and forms of entertainment – peep shows, strip tease, "vaginal coin-suck," "short/long time" and so on' (ibid., p. 26). Camptowns began with the Korean War and the arrival of US troops. The war created what Moon calls a 'supply of raw materials' in the form of girls and women affected by poverty and social chaos and millions of young orphans and widows. They fled towards the UN/US areas, which were mostly isolated in the countryside, and crime and gangsters went with them. Writing in 1997 she says that '[s]ince the war, over one million Korean women have served as sex providers for the U.S. military' (ibid., p. 1). Her book explores the relationship between the US military and Korean national and local governments that created the system and states: 'It is a system that is sponsored and regulated by two governments' (ibid.). 'Camptowns' were set up around the American bases, and their main business consisted of the clubs offering prostitution and the associated businesses that serviced the prostituted women and other employees. One camptown, American town, is described as 'completely isolated and walled off' and it has 'incorporated status'. It had a president and board of directors who managed all the businesses and the people living and working there. It was constructed in the early to mid-1970s from funds from local and national government. The board managed the apartments of the prostituted women and charged them rent. Some prostituted women were registered and others, mainly streetwalkers, not. Registration took place at the police station with the name of the club the women worked in. They had to pay to be examined at a clinic once a week, get VD cards showing their disease status and carry them at all times. The Korean Ministry of Health and Social Affairs supervised all of this.

As in the Philippines and other sites of US military prostitution in Asia, the registered women would sell drinks, dance with men and solicit prostitution buyers. They had to fondle the GIs and be fondled in order to sell the drinks. They had to be used sexually to acquire the bulk of their income at an hourly rate, in the mid-1980s, of $10, or $20 for overnight. The club owners and pimps took 80 per cent, with women getting the rest. Moon explains that how the women fared depended upon how the club owners and customers chose to behave. The worst that could happen was murder, with brutality such as a Coke bottle shoved into a woman's uterus and an umbrella in her rectum (ibid., p. 21). The women were in debt bondage and debts increased for medical treatment, through bribing police officers and through the adding on of all expenses. Debts were sometimes deliberately created so that women could not leave the clubs. The women entered military prostitution because they had already suffered severe deprivation and abuse, poverty, rape, domestic violence, rape by family members. Some were physically forced by traffickers and pimps who 'greeted young girls arriving from the countryside with promises of employment or room and board, then "initiated" them – through rape – into sex work or sold them to brothels' (ibid., p. 23).

There are considerable similarities with the prostitution system set up for the American military in the Philippines when it was occupied by the US following World War II. An agreement was made between the two governments called the Military Base Agreement, or MBA (Farr, 2004). This provided unhampered use of the Philippines for bases and other facilities for 44 years. In the Philippines prostitution around bases had the full support of the military, which organized the medical checks. The experiences of women abused by the US military in South East Asia were severe in the routine violence they entailed. Filipino women describe the favourite practice of their American prostitutors as 'three holes'. Women and bars were advertised to the servicemen as 'three-holers', meaning penetration of mouth, vagina and anus. One woman who was prostituted as a virgin for the first time at 14 said: 'I really didn't want to, but he forced me. It was very painful. He tried to undress me and I wouldn't get undressed. There was a lot of blood on my clothes' (Sturdevant and Stoltzfus, 1992, p. 80). Other practices that were required included boxing and wrestling so that the prostitutors could get sexually excited by seeing women in pain, and performing oral sex on groups of men under the tables in clubs. All of these practices are commonplace in the sex tourism which absorbed the prostituted women when the US military moved out, as we shall see in Chapter 6.

By the late 1960s, the Philippines was providing R&R with 55,000 prostituted women. When the agreement came to an end there was considerable public feeling in the Philippines against its renewal. When Clark Air Force Base, which spawned the prostitution town of Angeles City, and Subic Bay naval base, which obtained prostitution services from Olongapo, closed, the prostituted women in the base towns went to other military bases in Guam, Okinawa or Germany. Thousands were trafficked to Korea through the

Korean Special Tourism Association (KSTA), which served to bring 'entertainers' into the country to the camptowns. It was the *de facto* policy of the military to work with the KSTA for this purpose. In 1999, however, a new Visiting Forces Agreement was signed between the two governments despite considerable opposition from civil society organizations which objected to the creation of prostitution industries. This enabled the US military to use 22 ports for R&R, and Angeles City and Olongapo began to grow again.

Military prostitution made prostitution into a considerable market sector, to the extent that the country is now significantly dependent on the sex industry and prostitution trafficking. Kathryn Farr estimates the numbers of registered prostituted women in the Philippines in 2004 at 400,000, of whom one-quarter are underage, with the number of unregistered prostituted women unknown (Farr, 2004). When the troops left for the first time a gap in the market enabled a new set of entrepreneurs to set up. Americans, Australians and New Zealanders took ownership of bars and hotels through Filipino female partners, because foreigners were not allowed to own them, and created an industry of sex tourism (Jeffreys, 1999). More recently a new site of military prostitution has developed in the South of the Philippines in Zamboanga to service US troops sent to fight the threat of 'Islamic' terrorism in the area, and there are now an estimated 2,000 women and girls in prostitution compared with a mere handful before (Farr, 2004). Similar systems of US military prostitution were set up in Okinawa, in Hawaii, in Thailand and in Vietnam. Kathryn Farr sees military prostitution as just one form of what she calls 'congregational prostitution', a phenomenon that occurs wherever large groups of men live and work without their families. In such situations the women they are culturally empowered and expected to use are absent, and no community judgements act as a drag upon their sexual licence.

After military prostitution caused the industrialization of prostitution in a country, local women and girls became the raw materials of the global sex industry, not only prostituted within local and sex tourism industries at home but trafficked into prostitution worldwide. Thus in the 1980s and 1990s Thai women came to represent prostitution both to the sex tourists from rich nations who flocked into Thailand to use them sexually and in sex industries in Germany, Australia and Japan into which they were trafficked. Today Vietnamese women are trafficked into prostitution in Cambodia and Australia and many other countries. Korean women are increasingly trafficked to Australia (Fergus, 2005).

Peacekeeper prostitution: whose peace are they keeping?

Since the early 1990s another source for the development of prostitution industries has emerged in the form of the gathering of mostly men to engage in UN peacekeeping and reconstruction activities (Whitworth, 2004). It is an irony that not just militaries engaged in combat but also peacekeepers who are supposed to bring an end to the harms of combat should create prostitution systems in countries such as Cambodia, Kosovo, Liberia. The obvious question in relation to the prostitution of trafficked or local women and girls by peacekeepers is 'Whose peace are they keeping?', because though they may prevent some kinds of violence, they institute an abusive régime for many women. In conflict zones women and girls become vulnerable to prostitution as a result of being separated from families and being reduced to penury by displacement and destruction of subsistence. This vulnerability is easily exploited by 'peacekeepers' to add a new dimension of harm through sexual exploitation in return for survival. In some cases these gatherings of men create prostitution industries in areas where they have been barely in existence before their arrival, such as in Bosnia-Herzegovina and Kosovo (Harrington, 2005). In other cases where some form of prostitution industry already existed they have transformed this local practice into large-scale industries which require the trafficking of girls and women to provide supply. In some cases the peacekeepers, as in the Balkans, have been involved in trafficking themselves (ibid.). In Cambodia the arrival of UN peacekeeping troops caused the number of prostituted women and girls to rise from 1,500 to 20,000 in 1990 (Farr, 2004). In Mozambique in 1992 the prostitution industry had grown so large that a liaison officer was assigned to mediate between troops and prostitutes and traffickers. Peacekeepers created a prostitution industry in Rwanda in 1995. In West Africa, in Liberia, Guinea and Sierra Leone, women and girl children were forced into prostitution by peacekeepers and UN personnel in exchange for food and medicine. Peacekeeping and reconstruction are now very large-scale economic activities which, like mining, forestry or banana plantations, ruthlessly require and construct prostitution as an ordinary adjunct activity. As Carol Harrington puts it: 'Peacekeeping produces conditions for violence against women and girls in the sex industry by creating a lucrative market of buyers in highly paid militarized men' (Harrington, 2005, p. 176).

Harrington, however, does not condemn prostitution *per se*. In her work on Bosnia-Herzegovina and Kosovo she is careful to restrict her area of concern to 'violence in the sex industry'. She explains that peacekeeping is dominated by the military, and violence in the sex industry could not exist without the cooperation of locals and internationals in official positions. The men controlling the industry are former militia commanders from the area with the cooperation of local police. Though once they were rivals from different ethnic groups, they cooperate to make their living from trafficking and the earnings of prostitution. In the Balkans region, night clubs operate as 'confined brothels' and proliferated when the peacekeepers arrived. The women held captive within are foreign women in debt bondage and subject to considerable violence. They were often seeking to migrate to the west when trapped by traffickers. Though the clubs are off limits to the soldiers they still visit, and trafficked women have been taken onto army bases. The number of bars and clubs in Kosovo listed as off limits for soldiers because they were thought to be involved in trafficking gives an idea of the size of the problem of peacekeeper prostitution and trafficking in that country. Two hundred were listed in January 2004, which Harrington estimates as each having an average of nine women and girls, making a total of 1,800 prostituted women. The problem with Harrington being concerned specifically about 'violence' in peacekeeper prostitution is that it could be seen to create an unfortunate precedent, the normalizing of military prostitution when obvious 'violence' is not involved. This may be an example of the influence of the sex work position which can chill the usual condemnation that feminists might invoke towards this practice.

The NGO Refugees International named its report on sexual abuse by peacekeepers in the Democratic Republic of Congo, Liberia and Haiti after the remark by the UNTAC Missions' special representative in Cambodia in response to criticisms of the peacekeeper initiated sex industry there that 'boys will be boys' (Martin, 2005). The report points out the different ways in which peacekeepers sexually exploit local women and girls. In 2002 in Sierra Leone, humanitarian staff were found to be coercing sex from women and girls in refugee camps in exchange for subsistence (ibid.). In Eritrea, since 2000, there have been numerous reports of peacekeeper sexual exploitation and Italian, Danish and Slovak peacekeepers have been expelled for sex with minors. An Irish soldier was found to be making pornographic films of Eritrean women. Unfortunately it was the main female actor in the film who got punished with two years imprisonment whereas the peacekeeper himself got 16 days jail and was then dismissed. In 2003 Irish peacekeepers were reported to be prostituting girls as young as 15. The Refugees International report points out, usefully, that this behaviour of peacekeepers has much in common with sex tourism. In both cases men from richer countries find themselves free to play with the sexual exploitation of economically desperate girls, many very young, in poor countries.

In the early 2000s Thai women were being trafficked into brothels in East Timor, where peacekeeping and reconstruction forces created a thriving industry (Farr, 2004). In 2007 there continued to be revelations about the creation of a prostitution industry in East Timor to service UN peacekeepers and civilian staff there (Murdoch, 2007). Australian expatriates in Dili are reported as saying that the recent UN zero-tolerance policy towards sexual abuse and misconduct is being openly violated. A dozen brothels have recently opened and have UN vehicles parked outside most nights. One of the brothels has a dozen ethnic-Chinese women, which suggests that trafficking is already in place to supply the UN demand. The UN is reported to have received an internal report exposing a culture that has covered up abusive behaviour by UN staff in East Timor over years, including the fact that peacekeepers have left behind at least 20 babies they fathered to poor Timorese women. However, the UN spokeswoman in Dili is quoted as replying to these claims by saying the policy is being strictly enforced, with a special internal investigation unit being set up, which had received two reports of sexual abuse, but both cases had been closed for lack of evidence. The UN presence consists of 1,600 police and about 500 civilian workers.

Peacekeeper prostitution can take the form of marriage-like arrangements, i.e. sexual and domestic servicing for a period of time in return for subsistence or payment. This practice took place in Kosovo too. Some civilian peacekeepers took ownership of individual women for sex and housework by paying off their brothel debts. Others simply bought young teenage girls as sex slaves. Victor Malarek, in his account of trafficking and prostitution in the Balkans, comments upon an ethical peacekeeper's outrage when, in response to a dinner invitation from him and his wife, a co-worker arrived accompanied by a 14-year-old girl he had acquired in this way (Malarek, 2003). An Australian peacekeeper was accused of a similar practice in Sierra Leone (Sheil and Petrie, 2004). In this case Mandy Cordwell, a highly experienced Tasmanian police officer, reported and was the key witness in a case against a senior Victorian police superintendent, Peter Halloran, accused of sex crimes. Halloran was on unpaid leave, and Cordwell's boss in the war crimes unit of the United Nations-backed Special Court in Sierra Leone. Cordwell and her husband shared a house with Halloran, and she claimed that a 14-year-old girl, hired from her family as a maid, shared his bedroom overnight and made the bed in the morning. Halloran was cleared of the charge of sexual misconduct and returned to work in Victoria.

Prostitution in the form of marriage-like arrangements is common to sites in which military prostitution takes place. In the Philippines, as well in as other Asian military prostitution sites, servicemen sometimes paid a woman's debt to relocate her from bars and clubs into one-on-one prostitution/marriage until they were posted elsewhere. This form of relationship has commonly been a recourse of women forced to prostitute themselves in conflict zones, where attachment to one man affords some small protection against sexual use and abuse by many. It offers some element of control. Thus in her memoir of what was done to women in Berlin in 1945 when victorious Russian troops entered the city, the anonymous author of *A Woman in Berlin* describes how she would be claimed by a succession of individual soldiers who would return to use her sexually each day in exchange for food and alcohol, a practice which was better than gang rape by the multitude, though there was no real element of choice or power of refusal (Anonymous, 2005). In conflicts in Sierra Leone and Myanmar women and girls have been forced into sexual slavery and sometimes into marriage by rebel groups (Farr, 2004, p. 173). Refugees International points to the practice of 'bush wives' or sexual slaves being taken by combatants in Liberia and Sierra Leone (Martin, 2005). In Liberia, where, some reports state, the percentage of those who suffered sexual assault from combatants is as high as 60–70 per cent, being a 'bush wife' might be seen as a protected status.

Banning military and peacekeeper prostitution

As a result of the considerable unease that military and peacekeeper prostitution aroused in the international community, the increasingly obvious problem of trafficking and the prodding of women's rights organizations, two important developments took place in the 2000s to limit the damage. The scandal that arose from peacekeeper sexual exploitation, particularly of girls in refugee camps in return for food and survival in West Africa, caused new rules to be issued for peacekeepers by the UN in 2003 (United Nations, 2003). These rules forbid UN staff from having sexual relations with anyone under 18, the exchange of money, food or other privileges for sex, and 'strongly discourage' relations with beneficiaries, which means all members of host populations, on the grounds that they are based on inherently unequal power dynamics and undermine the credibility and integrity of the United Nations (Otto, 2007). In the US the Trafficking Victims Protection Reauthorization Act of 2005 amends the US military's Manual for Courts-Martial. Under the new Act, any service member convicted of patronizing a prostitute can receive a dishonourable discharge, forfeiture of all pay and allowances and one year of confinement. It is to be expected that the radical change of direction involved in directing US troops away from prostitution when they are so accustomed to see their prostitution behaviour as expected and condoned will not be achieved easily or quickly. There are some indications that there is no clear change as yet. Thus a 2006 report suggests that US servicemen at Yokosuka naval base in Japan are still using South Korean or Chinese, probably trafficked, 'massagy girls' a year after the change in military law made 'patronizing a prostitute' a specific offence (Batdorff and Kusumoto, 2006).

Surprisingly, the directive to UN staff has proved controversial in some circles, with even one feminist international law theorist arguing that it is a backward move (Otto, 2007). Dianne Otto is extremely critical of the fact that this policy bans staff from buying what she calls 'survival sex', which she says is a form of prostitution, from girls who are desperate for food and other privileges. She takes a sex work position towards this child prostitution and emphasizes the importance of the children's 'agency'. She starts her critique with examples of three girls, aged 13–17, who engage in survival sex in West African refugee camps. The 13-year-old does this to get scraps of food that will enable her to have the strength to look after her six-month-old baby. The directive, Otto considers, will wrongly deprive these girls of a means of survival. It is, she says, 'so out of step with the promotion of women's and children's rights' (ibid., p. 2, online version). Otto considers 'sex' to be innocent of harm. The problem for the girls is one of poverty rather than demonstrating any wrongful behaviour on the part of the UN staff, who might actually be trying to help. The directive is driven, she says, by 'sexual negativity' and a 'repressive politics of the body' and she references Gayle Rubin here (Rubin, 1984), a leading queer theorist of sadomasochism who takes a 'pro sex' position on prostitution and pornography. She points out that if payment is made for 'survival sex' it is 'often not even enough to buy a full meal' and there is always the risk of no payment at all. The girls, she acknowledges, had 'little or no power to negotiate the rate or to determine the kind of sexual exchange that took place, including whether safe sex was practiced' (Otto, 2007, p. 6). But this practice should not, she considered, be banned. The girls' 'stories' 'offer an opportunity to question overdetermined representations of powerlessness and to respect the rational calculations they are making ... but it is poverty that is the main harm, not sex' (ibid., p. 10). The preclusion of the activities covered in the directive 'drains agency' from those involved (ibid., p. 12). This is an example of the determination by some of those who take a sex work position to find 'choice' and 'agency' even in the most unlikely situations.

Military prostitution and civilian prostitution

There is a contradiction involved in seeking to prevent the clear harms to girls and women that are involved in military and peacekeeper prostitution whilst some governments, and even some feminist theorists and activists on prostitution, are arguing that legalization and decriminalization of civilian prostitution are the correct ways forward. Though the UN and American military prohibitions on prostitute use by servicemen and peacekeepers do not differentiate between sites in which prostitution is criminal, tolerated or legalized, it is reasonable to suppose that the prospective prostitutors might. Men reared in legalized environments such as the state of Nevada in the US, or the Eastern states of Australia, might find it hard to understand why prostitution that is understood as legitimate work and the exercise of women's agency in one place is a form of abusive practice in another. US sailors in Sydney or Melbourne might find it hard to understand why they should not use the legalized brothels, held up as world's best practice, that are available to them. Military prostitution cannot effectively be separated off from the ordinary civilian kind. Feminist theorists are much less likely to take a sex work or agency approach to military prostitution, though, as we have seen above in the work of Dianne Otto, some still do. This could be because the involvement of militaries and states is seen to overpower the exercise of women's agency and make an individualist approach less appropriate. Military prostitution may be an easier target of criticism because states and militaries can be held accountable, whereas in domestic contexts pinning down the culprits may require attacking the rights of men in general to prostitute women, and also bring confrontation with all the vested interests and forces of corruption that cause local sex industries to flourish.

The distinction between military and civilian prostitution could be seen to reproduce a public/private divide. Feminist theorists have shown that the idea that the public sphere is the proper realm of political theory and intervention, whilst the private sphere of the home, the family and intimate relationships is seen as not within the purview of real politics, is a dangerous one for women (Pateman, 1988; MacKinnon, 1989). Women and girls suffer the politics of male domination in the home, from doing housework for no pay whilst their brothers go skateboarding, for instance, to rape and violence from male family members. Feminist international politics theorists have usefully extended this understanding of the problem of the public/private divide to explain women's absence in person and in theory from international politics (Grant, 1991). The international stage can be seen as the 'public' stage, compared with domestic politics which represents the 'private'. Women, and feminist theory, have to bestride two huge barriers to become significant actors or have their concerns taken seriously within international politics. They have to get out, not only of the bedroom and the kitchen, but the boundaries of the nation as well. A concern with military prostitution which fails to connect it squarely with the problem of prostitution *per se* could be seen as replicating this unfortunate distinction. Through the lens of the public/private distinction, military prostitution can be identified as properly 'political', whereas domestic prostitution, even in Cambodia or Thailand, may be viewed as a matter of individual agency and not the concern of political theorists, particularly those involved with the important matters of relations between states. This sort of distinction between military and civilian prostitution could be seen as similar to the opposition between rape in marriage and 'stranger rape' that has afflicted legal practice. In civilian prostitution local men exercise rights to 'their women' when they prostitute them, whereas the prostitution of 'their women' by interlopers such as foreign militaries is a violation of ownership and of national boundaries and thus regarded as reprehensible.

Radical feminist theorists have made connections rather than distinctions in their approach to all areas of the sex industry and violence against women. Catharine MacKinnon, for instance, shows what the rape camps in Bosnia have in common with prostitution more generally. Of the Bosnian rape camps she writes: 'It is at once mass rape and serial rape indistinguishable from prostitution. It is concentration camp as brothel: women impounded to be passed around by men among men' (MacKinnon, 2006, p. 145). She says that '[w]artime is exceptional in that atrocities by soldiers against civilians are always essentially state acts' but 'men do in war what they do in peace' (ibid., p. 148). Radical feminist scholars seek explanations for rape and the prostitution of women in conflict zones in the cultures of misogyny and violence against women that the soldiers and their commanders were raised in. Liz Kelly expresses this idea succinctly in saying that 'sexual violence as a deliberate strategy in war and political repression by the state is connected in a range of ways to sexual violence in all other contexts' (Kelly, 2000, p. 45). In this understanding wartime rape and sexual exploitation are products of a pervasive climate of abuse of women. Ruth Seifert explains that the background to the rape orgies in Bosnia-Herzegovina was a culturally rooted contempt for women that is acted out with particular vehemence in times of crisis (Seifert, 1994). She employs this idea to explain how terrible atrocities against women came to take place, 'atrocities of a *quasi*-ritualistic character, whose core was the femaleness of the body. Thus, after being raped, women had their breasts cut off and their stomachs slit open' (ibid., p. 65). This behaviour is held down to some extent during peacetime by the possibility of social disapproval and let loose in times of social crisis when such controls no longer apply: 'women are raped not because they are enemies, but because they are the objects of a fundamental hatred that characterizes the cultural unconscious and is actualized in times of crisis' (ibid., p. 65).

Conclusion

This chapter has sought to draw connections between the everyday R&R prostitution carried out by the American military in Korea and the 'sexual slavery' of the comfort women system and the Bosnian rape camps. They share common features in the organization, recruitment and harms involved. All these systems create harms to the status of women and other social and political harms such as crime and corruption that are a regular part of prostitution industries in the countries in which they are practised. They may be distinguished by the extremity of the violence done to the women and the fact that in the Bosnian rape camps and in some areas of the comfort women system the women were not paid. Common to all these forms of prostitution is the idea that men have the right to access women for sexual use, an idea that is formed from cultures of misogyny and male dominance. This idea is the basis of domestic prostitution industries too. Many of the harms we have seen involved in military prostitution are common to domestic prostitution, because military systems are frequently built on traditional forms of prostitution. They are not distinct. This is an important issue because it is unlikely to be possible to effectively ameliorate the problems involved in military prostitution whilst men's sense of entitlement to use women in this way is developed through the toleration or legalization of civilian prostitution in their home countries. In Chapter 6 we examine the civilian prostitution tourism industry that was built out of the havoc that military prostitution created, and we will see the demobbed sexual warriors returning to the playgrounds of South East Asia and beyond.

Prostitution tourism
Women as men's leisure

The development of the sex tourism industry in Asia from the 1970s onwards was substantially aided by the groundwork put in place by US military prostitution. It began in the same sites in which prostitution had been developed to service the US military in rest and recreation, such as Thailand, the Philippines and Korea, and developed to the point where it was providing a substantial proportion of GDP in those countries. Indeed the governments of poor countries have deliberately developed sex tourism as a means to gain foreign exchange (Truong, 1990). But the sex industry grew strongly in other destinations in this period too, such as Amsterdam, Havana, Estonia, Jamaica, and needs to be explained in terms of other global forces. These include the development of the tourism industry and of consumption as a central engine of economic growth (Wonders and Michalowski, 2001). Sex tourism is a recent development, and an aspect of the development of tourism as an industry. Asian women caught up in the traffic in women in the east in the interwar period did not service occidental tourists as might happen in today's prostitution tourism, but went to foreign countries 'in search of clients among their own countrymen abroad' (League of Nations, 1933, p. 22). Nowhere were there found 'attempts to provide exotic novelty to brothel clients by offering them women of alien races' (ibid.).

The field of leisure studies has grown up in response to the developing importance of 'consumption' in the global economy. Currently sex tourism is being researched and taught as a legitimate aspect of 'leisure' in leisure and tourism studies (Opperman, 1998; Ryan and Hall, 2001). Consumption, leisure and tourism itself are all profoundly gendered, as feminist leisure studies researchers are pointing out (Deem, 1999). Women both facilitate men's leisure, through their unpaid work as housewives, and become the objects through which men achieve leisure, by being prostituted or acting as hostesses or strippers. Men's tourism stresses adventure and risk, and '[i]ncreasingly, women are themselves viewed as the destination' (Wonders and Michalowski, 2001, p. 551). Sex tourism has its apologists too in some women academics who write about the industry from a sex work perspective, stressing the agency of the prostituted women and arguing that sex tourism is not gendered, since women do it too, and does not require a feminist analysis (Kempadoo, 1998).

This chapter will examine this new 'leisure industry', looking at the way it is being normalized, its usefulness to male buyers and to business, and the serious harms to women that are integral to this exercise of the male sex right. I will argue that sex tourism outsources women's subordination, allowing tourists and businessmen from rich countries to access the greater desperation and degradation that can be bought in poor countries, or from trafficked women in cities like Amsterdam. It enables men in countries in which women are making advances towards equality, one aspect of which is the ability to deny men absolute sexual access, to buy women's sexual subordination elsewhere through their greater spending power. It offers white men the advantage of being able to purchase sexual fantasies of otherness and the notion that there are women elsewhere who are desperate for their touch.

Sex tourism is being increasingly recognized as important to regional and national economies. Tourism itself has grown hugely in importance in the world economy, so that in 1996 it formed 10 per cent of all consumer spending (Wonders and Michalowski, 2001, p. 549). As some poor countries have found themselves at a disadvantage in the new economic world order they have turned to tourism and expressly sex tourism as a way to gain dollar income: 'As newly industrializing countries struggle to find commodity niches in the globalized economy, they frequently find many of the best product niches taken. As a consequence, in some countries, sex tourism becomes a significant market fostering both national economic development and international capital accumulation' (ibid., p. 551). Ryan Bishop and Lillian Robinson, in their book on sex tourism in Thailand, do not seek to estimate what proportion of the worth of the tourism industry is attributable specifically to prostitution tourism, but clearly consider it significant when they say that '[a] $4 billion per year tourist industry is the linchpin of the modernization process called the "Thai Economic Miracle". And the linchpin of that industry is sex' (Bishop and Robinson, 1998). Cities in rich countries, too, are venturing into the promotion of sex tourism in order to compete for tourist numbers. Windsor in Canada legalized 'escort' prostitution, in a country where prostitution is illegal, in order to maximize the male tourists from the US who would come over the border to use its casinos and are important to the city's economy (Maticka-Tyndale et al., 2005). Though some commentators express deep unease at the development of prostitution tourism, others are more upbeat, saying that the economic worth of this industry should be recognized, and suggesting ways in which this can be enhanced (Singh and Hart, 2007).

I shall use the term 'prostitution tourism' rather than 'sex' tourism in this chapter for the sake of clarity. Though 'sex tourism' has generally been understood to be the behaviour of male tourists whose purpose is to engage in commercial sex with local women in tourist destinations (Enloe, 1989), it can have a wider application. The term does not necessarily imply prostitution and can potentially be used to apply to the behaviour of tourists who expect sexual interaction with fellow tourists in resorts, or non-commercial sex with locals or with other holidaying strangers in western destinations as a routine part of their holiday experience. The term 'sex tourism' is a euphemism, and a normalizing term, which can conceal the harm done by prostitution tourists and represent this form of men's behaviour as being about mutual fun and entertainment. The term 'prostitution tourism' is more suited to making the gendered nature of the phenomenon and its harms to women visible.

Prostitution tourism has not just developed in countries and sites in Asia that have harboured military prostitution. It is a developing part of the prostitution industry in all those areas where men as individuals or in groups travel for fun, on business, for sports events or political assemblies. They may be tourists visiting specially for the purpose of prostituting women, or to use casinos since prostitution use is integrally connected with this activity, or visiting businessmen, or male sports enthusiasts who prostitute women as an ordinary part of their travelling experience. There are prostitution tourism destinations in the rich world, such as Amsterdam and the US state of Nevada (Wonders and Michalowski, 2001; Shared Hope International, 2007; Farley, 2007). There are poor countries too that have used prostitution tourism as a tool to develop their economies and place local women in the marketplace as a resource to be exploited, without having profound experiences of military prostitution, such as Jamaica (Shared Hope International, 2007).

The Philippines

The Philippines provides a good example of prostitution tourism as it developed from the construction of a massive sex industry to service the American military bases (Santos *et al.*, 1998). It represents the variety of prostitution tourism in which rich men visit a poor country where they can access women as racialized others. Prostitution tourism in the Philippines has provoked intense campaigning by local and diaspora Filipino feminists to gain legislative change which would outlaw the practice. The report of a study tour to show Australians how prostitution tourism works characterizes these harms well:

> the sex tourism industry matters. It is big, it is wealthy, and it is damaging. It thrives on the poverty of the Philippines, and on the racism and sexism that exists in Australia, New Zealand and the Philippines. It exposes women and girls to violence and humiliation, and leaves them in it, day after day, year after year, until it has no further use for them. It paints a picture of the Philippines as a nation of available, submissive women, who can be fucked, beaten, married, discarded, divorced, killed.
>
> (Distor and Hunt, 1996, p. 3)

Prostitution tourism has been promoted by the government in the Philippines because of its profitability. Income generated by visitor arrivals in 1993 was US$2.12 billion, and 63.7 per cent of tourists were men (Distor and Hunt, 1996).

Angeles City, for instance, owes its existence to the servicing, including through prostitution, of the Clark Air Force Base. When the Americans withdrew there was a hiatus in the sex industry in the city which was quickly filled by Australian entrepreneurs and Australian sex tourists. At least 80 per cent of the 152 nightclubs and other entertainment spots were owned and operated by Australians in 1995. There are no beaches or views in Angeles City, only prostitution, and almost all hotels and bars are devoted to that end. Australians formed the largest number out of the 120,000 tourists who visited the area in 1994. Agencies in Australia arrange package tours for sex tourists to the city, amongst other destinations. The majority of the women in the bars servicing sex tourists are very young, some barely teenagers, sometimes playing cat's cradle when not needed by male buyers or having to dance on the stage where they get chosen (Jeffreys, 1999). Prostitution tourism in the Philippines works through the provision of a companion for the entire holiday or/and the buying of women and girls in bars through the payment of bar fines. The bars service different socioeconomic segments of men. Those servicing Japanese and Taiwanese sex tourists are the most expensive and luxurious. The next layer services European and Australasian tourists. The lowest level of bar, which might have no sanitation, services working class Filipino men. The tourist selects a girl and asks to buy her a 'ladies' drink' so that she will sit with him at a table. Men who so desire can buy the woman for the night or for the day by paying a bar fine to the bar cashier, of which half would go to the girl. Women's NGOs in the Philippines and Filipino expatriates in the countries which send prostitution tourists are working to end the practice because it harms generations of Filipino women who are caught up in prostitution and because it harms the status of Filipino women in general. Campaigns by the Coalition Against Trafficking in Women Asia Pacific (CATWAP) and other organizations led to the passing of a far-reaching anti-trafficking law in 2003. This legislation, which penalizes those who 'maintain or hire a person to engage in prostitution or pornography', specifically targets prostitution tourism, making it an offence to '[t]o undertake or organize tours and travel plans consisting of tourism packages or activities for the purpose of utilizing and offering persons for prostitution, pornography or sexual exploitation' (see www.catw-ap.org). The prostitution tourism destination of Amsterdam has a very different history, but it is also facing growing opposition from politicians and citizens who want to reduce the presence of the industry in the city.

The Netherlands

The Netherlands represents a different kind of sex tourism destination, not just because it is a city in a rich country, but because the sex tourists are most likely to be using the resource of trafficked women, who have been removed from their countries of origin to service rich men elsewhere, rather than local women who may have alternatives to being prostituted for their survival. An estimated 75 per cent of the women in windows prostitution in Amsterdam in the 1990s were foreign women, and this form of prostitution is particularly directed at tourists (Wonders and Michalowski, 2001). As Wonders and Michalowski put it in their study of prostitution tourism in Amsterdam and Havana: 'In Amsterdam, the commodification of bodies has been perfected to the level of an art form' so that the red light district resembles a 'shopping mall' with 'windows and windows of women to choose from' (ibid., p. 553). It became a 'sex tourist's Mecca' (ibid.) as a result of a history of toleration of prostitution and drug use and easy access to these commodities. Many businesses in the city that service the sex tourists are now dependent upon the revenues they get from this source, such as hotels, strip clubs and the sex museum. The Netherlands has 13 official red light districts, which are well suited to a prostitution tourism industry. Apart from windows prostitution there are a variety of clubs in which prostitution is readily accessed. Interestingly, these clubs operate in a similar way to those in the Philippines, in that the male buyers must order drinks and can request girls for conversation, and then pay if they wish to penetrate the woman (Shared Hope International, 2007). This may suggest that the practices of prostitution are being disseminated worldwide as tourists and pimps circulate in the global economy of prostitution. There are some local teenage girls in windows prostitution for tourists to access too. They are inducted into the industry at an average age of 15½ years, and controlled by 'loverboy' pimps of Turkish and Moroccan origin (ibid.; UNHRC, 2007b). They carry tattoos of their pimps' names on their arms. Amsterdam Councillor Roel van Duijn of the Green Left Party says that there are over 10,000 prostituted women in Amsterdam and only about 2,000 are employed legally. The rest are in the illegal industry, which is 'rife with sex slavery' (Shared Hope International, 2007).

So famous, and normalized, has Amsterdam become as a prostitution tourist destination that in 2005 the major UK travel company Thomas Cook initiated a walking tour of the red light district which was open to all ages (Shared Hope International, 2007). The tour included a stop at the Prostitution Information Centre. There was some outrage amongst locals who objected to the company permitting and encouraging minors to participate through cost incentives. Adult tickets for the tour, for instance, cost £12, whilst children's tickets cost only £6 and tickets for under threes were free. In December 2005 the company removed the offensive tour description but other tour operators still promote and host walking tours with 'adults only' restrictions. There has been some disillusionment about Amsterdam's prostitution industry since legalization in 1999, which was supposed to clean up the associated crime and trafficking, because these problems have markedly increased and the city government has found it necessary to close down one-third of the windows in Amsterdam as a result (Hesen, 2007; Moore, 2007). Also citizens and business organizations have become uneasy about the way that prostitution tourism represents their city. Buildings in the main windows district are being requisitioned and turned into clothing boutiques.

The normalization of prostitution as leisure

For the discipline of leisure studies, prostitution tourism is most usually proclaimed to be a satisfying form of leisure activity for the prostitutors and an ordinary form of work for those who are prostituted, but plagued by a few problems, such as child prostitution and violence, that can be cleared up by legalizing the industry. Leisure studies approaches do not generally recognize that there is anything gendered about prostitution tourism. Thus Martin Opperman, in a collection which lays out the field of 'sex' tourism as an area of leisure studies, comments in relation to businessmen engaged in prostitution tourism: 'With the increase in female executives, the reversed sex roles may also become more common' (Opperman, 1998, p. 16). There is a gap in the analysis here, since there are no men and boys dancing on stages to be chosen by 'women', and that needs to be explained as more than an absence of equal opportunities for women. Contributors to the volume all take the position that prostitution needs to be legitimized as ordinary work. Joan Phillip and Graham Dann argue that women prostituted in tourism related bars in Bangkok should be recognized as 'entrepreneurs', involved in the ordinary risk taking activities associated with business enterprise, in a manner which blithely disappears the gender dimension and the harms of the practice: 'Prostitution is simply another form of entrepreneurship' (Phillip and Dann, 1998, p. 70). These risks, they say, include not getting paid and still having to pay off the bar fine to the bar owner, violence which can lead to death, health problems such as AIDS, and male buyers who take condoms off as soon as the lights go off. But these 'risks' that are integral to prostitution are seen as the woman's responsibility: 'Risk taking involves bearing responsibility for one's actions' (ibid., p. 66). They say that the women need, like any entrepreneur, to make decisions, and the main one is which male buyers to accept, i.e. which ones are murderous and which are not: 'Decision making is a function of skill' and '[t]he skill needed to reduce that element of chance is defined as entrepreneurial' (ibid.).

Stripping is seen as a leisure or 'tourist' activity by some leisure studies researchers. Male leisure studies academics in particular seem to have some difficulty empathizing with the actual experience of strippers and allow their own identities as male voyeurs to get in the way. Thus Donlon, who identifies all men who go to strip clubs as 'participants in touristic episodes' (Donlon, 1998, p. 116), describes women who are looking about to identify men who might be interested enough to tip them well, whilst they are dancing, thus: 'The procedure may be likened to a skilful predator casting about for prey' (ibid., p. 120). He proceeds to make his identification with what he sees as the poor beleaguered buyer rather than the stripper even clearer: 'For the duration of the club visit, entertainers are certainly freely ogled, with little or no feigned concern for this gaze, and yet are largely in power. Clients are, conversely, forced to operate in a direct *quid pro quo* relationship, entirely based on commercial exchange' (ibid., p. 121). Donlon specializes in studying 'controversial' leisure such as cock fighting as well as stripping. Two other male leisure studies professors who take a similarly gender biased approach are Ryan and Hall (2001). They specifically reject feminist criticism of sex tourism and prostitution in scathing tones. They say that 'much of the debate on sex tourism ... has been hijacked by a feminist rhetoric within which the client is the male and the prostitute female ... It also implies that the prostitute is the victim' (Ryan and Hall, 2001, p. 37).

Another very positive perspective from the leisure studies field is the work of Singh and Hart, who argue that prostitution tourism should receive recognition as a 'cultural industry'. They say that '[n]aming sex work as a cultural industry will lead to effective policies that ... accord it status' (Singh and Hart, 2007, p. 170). They say that organizations such as the World Trade Association and the World Tourism Organization are 'working with the developing world to promote cultural policies – often linked to cultural industries such as tourism' (ibid., p. 156). This will enable developing countries to increase their share of the sex tourism market. They explain that in 2004, whilst globally international tourism arrivals numbered 763 million and were worth $623 billion, the developing world received less than 20 per cent of the arrivals and receipts. Creating the idea that prostitution is a 'cultural industry', they consider, will help to right this inequality. They say that the cultural industries usually recognized are about the performing and creative arts rather than prostitution but prostitution should be included. Foreign tourists, they say, go to Thailand to access prostituted women for a distinct cultural experience. They could, after all, use prostituted women in their home countries without the costs of travel if all they were concerned with is cheapness. One of the 'cultural' differences they offer is that: 'Thai women are described as tender and nurturing, offering companionship to their clients, not just sex' (ibid., p. 161). This could also be seen as showing more desperation for money which occasions greater subservience, but this is not their understanding. Singh and Hart conclude that the idea that 'sex work' should be 'shut down' is a facile solution. Though there are problems connected with it such as trafficking, dehumanization and racism, these can be dealt with individually whilst preserving the industry of prostitution itself because the 'answer lies in reform, and monitoring of abusive practices, not in shutting down the industry altogether' (ibid., p. 170). Unfortunately, this sex work perspective also dominates the considerable body of work in which feminist researchers have mapped the forms and practices of prostitution tourism in the last decade (Kempadoo, 1999a, 2004; Kempadoo and Doezema, 1998).

The sex work approach to sex tourism in feminist theory

Feminist researchers who take a sex work approach differ from the completely uncritical researchers above in analysing the class and race dimensions of the practice. They take a Marxist and postcolonial perspective and explain that 'sex' tourism is a good illustration of the global flows of inequality. The feminist commentators explain that tourism destinations are formed, as in the Caribbean, from colonial oppression. In the neo-colonial practice of sex tourism, rich, often white and western men choose to visit poor countries to sexually use women who must prostitute to survive. They show

how 'sex' tourism operates as a service sector for the capitalist west, refreshing tired corporate warriors in a form of 'rest and recreation' similar to that created for US soldiers in South East Asia (Jyoti Sanghera, 1997). Kemala Kempadoo explains that prostitution tourism props up 'corporate capital, First World identities, and masculine hegemony' (Kempadoo, 1999b, p. 18).

Prostitution tourism offers men from rich countries the opportunity to confirm their masculine dominance over women, who are claiming equality in the west and prepared neither to accept masculine authority nor to adapt themselves so dutifully to men's sexual demands. As Kempadoo puts it: 'Many male sex tourists ... expressed the view that in their home countries, women enjoy excessive power, through which traditional male authority is being undermined ... In the Caribbean, they are able to fully reaffirm their masculinity' (ibid., p. 26). However, Kempadoo takes a sex work approach and positions the prostituted women and men of the Caribbean as having 'agency' and being involved in acts of transgression which free them from oppressive relations rather than subjecting them to oppression. Too many studies, she considers, emphasize the problems associated with prostitution, and obscure the 'agency and subjectivity' of sex workers (Kempadoo, 2001, p. 41).

Though this feminist work shows an acute awareness that prostitution tourism is based on class, race and gender inequality, it takes the position that recognizing prostitution as work and legalizing it will resolve the problems associated with the practice. Beverley Mullings, for instance, writing about Jamaica, says that if 'paid sexual labor' is not recognized as 'legitimate work' then the sex workers will be vulnerable to labour and human rights abuses (Mullings, 1999). Sex tourism should, she says, 'be viewed as an export industry, with consumers who import services from local providers' (ibid., p. 57). Taking this 'industry approach' will allow the 'truly exploitative aspects' to be 'more effectively policed' (ibid., p. 79). 'Sex' tourism can then take on the character of a 'truly community-based tourism' (ibid., p. 79). In fact studies of the states in which prostitution has been recognized as work and the industry has been legalized do not support the notion that this approach will reduce the harms of prostitution (Farley, 2007; M. Sullivan, 2007; Shared Hope International, 2007). The field research and interviews of feminist prostitution tourism researchers, whether they take a sex work perspective or not, provide good support for the notion that prostitution tourists from the rich western world seek to compensate hemselves for the loss of masculine status they experience from an increase in women's equality.

Motives of prostitution tourists

Women's emancipation caused a great deal of angst to men at the start of the 20th century, and some of those who were bestriding the empire as administrators or traders were able to reassure themselves through the prostitution of Asian women. Thus this wail of complaint, from a 1928 book by a European man on the perils of feminism, demonstrates an infuriation with western, more emancipated women, which will be translated later in the century, after another wave of feminist activism, into an impulse towards prostitution tourism:

> he who knows how terrible and degrading it can be, especially to a nobler masculine nature, to be reduced to mating with one of the numerous sexually anaesthetic white women, will understand the European returned from the tropics, who replies to the experts' enquiries that he prefers the Malayan, Polynesian or Japanese mistress, who screamed with joy if he only laid his hand on her, to the icy white woman, who regarded his erotic transports with contempt and did not even shrink from showing him that she only just bore with him because it was supposed to be part of her wifely duties. And to make things worse, she wronged her husband in this by a feeling that precisely by doing so she showed herself a 'higher being' than he, though, of course, the truth is that she is a defective individual, a poor invalid, a presumptuous ignoramus in matters of love.
>
> (Knudsen, 1928, p. 111)

Weith Knudsen's words are taken from a book in which he complains generally about the emancipation of women, which clearly caused him considerable displeasure. In this earlier time the colonial adventurers who discovered the joys of sexually using Asian women were engaged on the business of the empire rather than holidaying.

In the late 20th century, a study found similar motivations on the part of male Australian prostitution tourists. It reports that 'a variety of factors have converged to endanger the individual's sense of his place in the world' (Kruhse-MountBurton, 1995, p. 199), such as smaller families, wives who work for payment and a reduction in women's willingness to do housework. In relation to sex, men's ideal of the passive woman, which allowed them to see themselves as teachers and initiators, has been undermined by women's expectation of sexual pleasure. Even prostitution behaviour in Sydney, Australia, whose red light district is a hangover from the servicing of the US military in the Vietnam War, is unsatisfactory because the prostituted women are seen as being 'emotionally and sexually cold ... making little effort to please' and as failing to 'disguise the commercial nature of the interaction' (ibid., p. 193). Also prostituted women in Australia may demand safe sex, restrict the practices they are prepared to offer, and may not be sufficiently young for the men's taste. Prostitution tourism reaffirms their superior status as men and reassures them against the troubling 'changing role of women', which 'appears to have posed a considerable threat to the male identity' (ibid., p. 202).

O'Connell Davidson's work on male sex tourists to Thailand demonstrated that they were all strongly motivated by the opportunity to 'live like kings' or 'playboys' (O'Connell Davidson, 1995, p. 45). The men experienced pleasures ranging from the acquisition of mail order brides through 'the mere pleasure of looking at sexually available women [and men and children], at one pole to the satisfaction of complete sexual possession at the other' (ibid., p. 46). These pleasures are illustrated by a bar in Pattaya called the 'No Hands Bar', where prostituted women 'crawl under the tables in order to fellate the customers' (ibid.). The men O'Connell Davidson interviewed were not just angry at European prostitutes but had what she calls a 'misogynistic rage' at western women in general for acting as though they are men's equals and not worshipping them as kings. The rage is at 'women who have the power to demand anything at all, whether it is the right to have a say over who they have sex with and when, or the right to maintenance payments for their children' (ibid., p. 53). 'Sex tourism', says O'Connell Davidson, 'helps British men to reinforce and construct a powerful and positive image of themselves as a particular kind of white heterosexual man' (ibid., p. 52).

The male sex tourists gain enhanced masculine status from demonstrating their sexual use of local women to their mates. O'Connell Davidson explains one motivation for male sex tourists in the Dominican Republic to make sexual use of local women is that it 'provides the basis for recognition and acknowledgement between men' (O'Connell Davidson, 2001, p. 16). She quotes a male sex tourist saying that in his hotel which is '95% single men' they achieved 'great comradery' by discussing their sexual use of local women. She comments that 'women serve to reproduce social links between the male members of the community' (ibid., p. 19). Sex tourism for men helps to cement the male bonding which is an important component of male dominance. This male bonding can be achieved through the 'stag' weekends offered to young British men in Eastern Europe (CBS News, 2005), in which 1,200 groups of men descend on Prague yearly to partake of the pleasures of sexual entertainment', cause distress to local people and get barred from restaurants for their destructive behaviour.

Business and sports prostitution tourism

Male bonding of this kind is becoming more and more central to business networking internationally, and this practice excludes businesswomen. An article in the *Economist* in 2005 comments on the three main explanations that top business women in America give for why so few of them get to the highest level. The first of these involves the sex industry: 'First comes exclusion from informal networks. In many firms jock-talk and late-night boozing still oil the wheels of progress. In America and elsewhere it has become almost traditional for sales teams to take potential clients to strip clubs and the like. These activities specifically exclude most women' (*Economist*, 2005). This is particularly true of business conducted in Asian markets. Research on British women executives on international assignments has shown that they face 'greater problems with adaptation in traditionally patriarchal cultures' (Forster, 1999). Those working in China and Japan, for instance, were much more likely to report difficulties with cultural adaptation and to face specific obstacles and prejudices. One reason is likely to be the common practice of mixing business with prostitution.

The practice of providing prostitution as an ordinary accompaniment to business has been strongly developed in Japan. A 2007 report on prostitution tourism in Japan gives some details of how this operates. The Japanese mafia, the Yakuza, organize sex cruises in the Maldives for Japanese businessmen and foreign nationals (Shared Hope International, 2007, p. 131). Corporate after-hours socializing tends to be done with entertainers and prostitutes (ibid., p. 135). The practice is not new in the west, though it may, until recently, have been less common as prostitution was less normalized as a practice. Today western corporations provide prostituted women to valued international guests. The biggest escort agency in Australia, Royalty Services, which has an annual turnover of $20 million, provides 'escorts with modelling backgrounds to clients for negotiable prices ranging from $5000 per night to $130,000 per month' (IBISWorld, 2007, p. 23), with 'the bulk of business being visiting businessmen being entertained by corporations attempting to gain their custom'.

Business prostitution becomes particularly important to the economies of cities that rely heavily on business conventions, such as Atlanta. As a report on sex tourism and trafficking to that city explains, there is '[a]ggressive marketing of the city to organizers of conventions and sporting events' (Shared Hope International, 2007, p. 104). This is necessary because Atlanta, like other cities that are lured into creating massively expensive and subsequently useless sports infrastructure to service the masculine culture of competitive sport, has 'cavernous venues constructed for the Olympic games of 1996' which it needs to fill. Sports prostitution tourism is in itself an important and growing driver of prostitution markets. The IBISWorld report on the prostitution industry in Australia announces that sporting events such as the motor racing Grand Prix in Melbourne cause huge increases in the demand for prostitution from overseas and interstate visitors (IBISWorld, 2007). The Atlanta Convention and Visitors Bureau reported 2005 convention attendance numbers at 3,105,256 people, attending 3,068 conventions averaging 3.4 days each. This creates considerable income for the city. Though women doubtless were in attendance, most of the visitors were expected to be men. In Atlanta advertisement cards are handed out to convention attendees promising VIP treatment at the various 'gentlemen's clubs' in the area. Discount entry cards are also distributed at sporting events, concerts and other entertainments. Men's prostitution behaviour is such an integral part of these jamborees that '[o]ne major hotel's courtesy guest shuttle was observed providing transportation for guests to a strip club, further facilitating the commercial sex markets' (ibid., p. 104).

The city of Sydney, Australia, where brothels are legal, experienced a prostitution boom when the Asia-Pacific Economic Cooperation (APEC) summit took place in 2007. The male buyers were mostly secret service agents and international trade envoys.

Business went up by 300 per cent (*Sun-Herald*, 2007). The varieties of sexual abuse of prostituted women on offer reveal a worrying lack of respect for women: 'Interstate prostitutes were brought in to fill demand at the city's establishment, where APEC-themed specials such as the Condi Combo, the UN Duo and the Presidential Platter were on offer.' The 'United Nations Duo' comprised time with 'two girls of different ethnicities' (Ahmed, 2007). Such practice harms the equality of women in the international delegations and the possibility of women's issues being fairly discussed at such meetings.

Business prostitution has become a significant problem in China since the introduction of the market economy (Zhou, 2006). Traditional forms of prostitution, too, have been revived and diversified and new forms have been introduced in a good example of the ways in which capitalist economic development currently uses women's bodies as a basic but unspoken resource. Some Chinese companies advertise jobs for beautiful young women under 25 as Public Relations Officers', which is often synonymous with being prostitutes employed by the companies for high-ranking executives, potential clients and company partners (ibid.). Hong Kong and Taiwanese men who work in China are able to exploit the severe poverty of mainland Chinese women who migrate to the special economic zones, such as Shenzhen, to find work (Hobson and Heung, 1998). A flourishing prostitution industry has developed to service visiting businessmen. A Hong Kong magazine reported that 'five or six "porn stables" have been set up in the lounges of Shenzhen hotels. The prostitutes, known as female "horses", have to pay HK$50 (US$7) entrance fee. The men then pay HK$200 (US$25) to take a horse to their table, additional services at the horse's table cost upwards of HK$750 (US$100)' (ibid., p. 137). There are also 'luxurious yellow "sex tour" coaches' available, 'with female tour guides who are available to provide sexual services to the guests while they are on the bus' (ibid.). The customers are from Hong Kong, Taiwan and Japan. The harmful traditional practice of concubinage, however, is particularly common amongst working class truck drivers. In either case it is problematic for the men's wives, 41 per cent of whom said they would divorce their husbands if they found out. As a radio talk show put it in Hong Kong: 'In HK they might be a truck driver or even a street sweeper, with no status. But, when they go across the border to their concubines they get treated like gods' (quoted in Hobson and Heung, 1998, p. 140).

One problematic aspect of the normalization of prostitution tourism practices is that a sizeable proportion of girls involved in the local prostitution industries that tourists access are children.

Child prostitution tourism

The positive picture of prostitution tourism which is given in the leisure studies literature is bedevilled by one difficult reality, which is that a large proportion of those used in the industry are girls under 18 years old. In the last two decades, during which prostitution tourism has developed very considerably as a market sector, there has been increasing concern in the international community about 'child sex tourism' (Jeffreys, 2000a). As is the case with 'child' prostitution and 'child' pornography, children are separated out from the rest of the global sex industry as special objects of concern. This distinction is visible in the work of the international NGO End Child Prostitution in Asian Tourism (ECPAT) and in the Protocol to the 1999 UN Convention on the Rights of the Child, which deals specifically with the sexual exploitation of children in prostitution and pornography. In relation to 'child sex tourism' governments have passed special extraterritorial legislation so that they can prosecute on return their nationals who have sexually exploited children overseas (Hall, 1998; Seabrook, 2000; Jeffreys, 2002). These organizations and international instruments distinguish the harms of prostitution according to age. They use the age of 18, as in the children's convention, as a cut-off point, seeing prostitution from the 18th birthday onwards as potentially freely chosen, agentic prostitution with which they should have no concern, whereas prostitution up to the day before this birthday is seen as physically and emotionally harmful and morally repugnant.

In fact 'child' prostitution is hard to distinguish from the rest of the prostitution industry, as an ILO report shows (Lim, 1998). In one major brothel complex in Indonesia, 10 per cent of workers were below 17 and, of those 17 and above, 20 per cent became prostitutes under 17. A 1994/5 survey of Indonesia's registered prostitutes found 60 per cent aged 15–20 (ibid., p. 7). In Malaysia, of the women and girls rescued by police from brothels between 1986 and 1990, 50 per cent were under 18 and the rest 18–21 (ibid., p. 173). A Thai study found that 20 per cent of prostituted women and girls started working between 13 and 15 (ibid.). The clear conclusion from such statistics would seem to be that prostitution is based upon the exual use of very young women or girls in poor countries. Tourism exacerbates the problem of child prostitution but the children are already integrated into the home-grown prostitution industry.

Some feminist commentators have questioned the distinction between child and adult prostitution. I have argued, for instance, that the harms identified as arising from the prostitution of children replicate quite precisely the harms that have been identified in adult prostituted women (Jeffreys, 2000a). Julia O'Connell Davidson also argues against the usefulness of the distinction (O'Connell Davidson, 2005). She points out that teenage girls are fully integrated into systems of prostitution in many parts of the world. She explains that though there is a demand from men specifically interested in prostituting young children, a.k.a. paedophiles, this is a small and specialist market. The majority of prostitution abusers are indigenous men and both they and prostitution tourists use teenagers in prostitution as a routine part of their prostitution abuse, neither seeking children nor, in many cases, recognizing or remarking the extreme youth of those they abuse. Though O'Connell Davidson and I both criticize the distinction, it is with different intent. Whereas I argue that NGOs and feminist theorists should be aiming to end the prostitution of all women and girls if they are serious about ending child sexual exploitation, because child prostitution cannot effectively be separated out, O'Connell Davidson takes a different path. She says she is 'uncomfortable with what I view as a more general impulse to separate children out as a special case' and with what she calls '[t]his process of ranking' which evinces 'outrage at child prostitution' (O'Connell Davidson, 2005, p. 1). But she criticizes what she calls 'anti-prostitution feminists', who, she says, ignore the 'diverse and complex realities' of those who are prostituted and deny their 'autonomy and agency' (ibid., p. 3). Through stressing that children can have 'agency', she joins a growing stream of feminist researchers who are arguing that both children and adult women express agency and choice in prostitution, and that showing special concern for children infantilizes them.

Since such a large proportion of those being used by the global sex industry are young teenage girls, the normalization of their participation is necessary if the global sex industry is to be legitimated and continue its growth unhindered. Some writers, even in feminist anthologies, are prepared to support this normalization. Thus Heather Montgomery, for instance, writing about prostituted children in a tourist resort in Thailand, says that children's 'agency' needs to be acknowledged (H. Montgomery, 1998). She says that arguments that prostitution damages children are ethnocentric. Treena Rae Orchard argues that girls in devadasi prostitution in India, who are given to priests to be brought up as prostitutes in an act which historically was supposed to show religious devotion but is now engaged in by families so that they can live on the daughter's income, should not be understood as 'victimized' (Orchard, 2007). The practice, she says, has positive aspects. The girls gain in status because they are important economically in their families and surrounded by networks of friends, despite the fact that they do not want to be prostituted and their virginity is auctioned off to the highest bidder at 14 or younger.

The argument that child prostitution in situations where it is practised by whole tribes, such as the 'untouchables', or among the people who practise devadasi prostitution, gives girls status is not borne out by other accounts. A report in the *Guardian* on child prostitution among dalit or untouchable tribes in Madhya Pradesh explains that girls are put into prostitution from 10–14 years old by the Baccharas and the Bedia (Prasad, 2007). Girls are hawked to buyers along the highways, with violence against the girls from clients and families being common. An example is given of a girl who was delivered to a food shack run by her uncle on a highway at 12. All the money she earned was taken by her family and used to build a new house with a room for each of four sons and to pay for the sons' marriages. Her low status as a girl was not, in this case, alleviated by the fact she provided most of the family income. Indeed the status of women is not necessarily high in other situations where they supply income to pimps/partners in western prostitution.

Do women do it too?

Another difficulty for those seeking to justify prostitution tourism as sex work and the expression of agency is the rather obviously gendered nature of the practice. To get around this problem some prostitution tourism researchers and theorists have taken to stressing that 'women do it too', generally in the form of western women having sex with 'beach boys' in the Caribbean. This 'sex tourism' by women, they argue, shows that prostitution is not fundamentally gendered, and it is reasonable to downplay feminist analysis and concentrate on race and class perspectives (Kempadoo, 1998;

O'Connell Davidson, 2005; Sanchez Taylor, 2001). These writers use the existence of 'female sex tourism' to argue that women can be just as exploitative as men, so that, were it not for the restrictions on the construction of sexuality created by patriarchy, women would be as likely to use men and women in prostitution as men. Jacqueline Sanchez Taylor accuses 'radical feminists' such as Cynthia Enloe and myself of promoting misleading stereotypes of sex tourists. She says that we are wrong to portray sex tourists as men, rather than persons of both sexes, and wrong to 'treat sex tourism and prostitution as first and foremost an expression of male patriarchal power and female powerlessness' (Sanchez Taylor, 2001, p. 749). This approach degenders prostitution. A careful analysis of the differences between the 'sex tourism' of women and that of men, however, shows profound variations in power, effects, consequences and meanings as a result of the different positions of the actors in the sex class hierarchy.

The similarities that those who seek to include women point to are the economic and racial privileges of both male and female western tourists in comparison with their local sexual partners. Western tourists are seen as being motivated by racist sexual stereotypes and using sex tourism to bolster their privileged race and class status. Female sex tourists, such researchers say, employ fantasies of otherness in the same way male sex tourists do, in their interaction with black men in the Caribbean. The women are looking for 'black men with good bodies, firm and muscle-clad sex machines that they can control, and this element of control should not be overlooked' (O'Connell Davidson and Sanchez Taylor, 1999, p. 51). Another similarity is the fact that the women 'sex' tourists and some of the men claim that they are not engaging in prostitution at all, but romance (Pruitt and LaFont, 1995; Dahles and Bras, 1999). Research on male sex tourists suggests that though some men visit destinations such as Thailand with the expectation that they will pay prostituted men and women for sex, others are naïve enough to believe that they are not engaging in prostitution behaviour (O'Connell Davidson, 1995). The women they engage with are skilled at not making their financial demands clear so that such men can remain deluded as to the nature of the relationships (Seabrook, 2001). It is surprising that the male tourists are so naïve considering that men are aware that a prostitution script exists for relations between men and women. The prostitution and pornography industry, as well as the tales of their mates, exist to make them aware of this. For women there is no such script. The purchase of sex from men plays no part in the culture that women inhabit and there is no reason that they should be aware of this possibility.

The differences between the behaviour of male and female sex tourists are numerous. They are clearest in the forms of sexual and romantic interactions which take place between women tourists and Caribbean men. The scale of 'female sex tourism' is rather different from that of male sex tourism. Julia O'Connell Davidson says that 'heterosexual female sex tourism is, in numerical terms, a far, far smaller phenomenon than male sex tourism' (O'Connell Davidson, 1998, p. 81). Most of the differences arise from the different positions in the sex class hierarchy that the women and men tourists occupy. The sexuality of men under male dominance is constructed to confirm their masculinity through practices of objectification and aggression (Jeffreys, 1997). The clearest expression of this sexuality of dominance lies in the existence of the sex industry which both reflects and helps to shape it. Women's sexuality, constructed out of a position of powerlessness, tends to be expressed in very different ways. There is no street or brothel prostitution of men and boys for women to access in any sex tourist destinations. This might suggest that whilst men's sex tourism is simply the extension of already existing systems of prostitution that exist for men to access prostituted others, women's 'sex tourism' is an altogether different phenomenon, with little relationship to prostitution.

One principle that distinguishes the sexuality of prostitution is that the prostituted women service the men sexually without any sexual pleasure on their part, and with the men firmly in control of the action. It is notable that women 'sex tourists' also end up servicing male sexuality. One Barbadian beach boy interviewed for Joan Phillip's study explained his sexual enthusiasm for women tourists thus: 'Bajan women can't fuck, and they doan even wanta suck you. You got to beg she to do it, and still she might not do it, and if she do it she acting like if she doin you a favor. Now a white woman, you gotta beg she to stop!' (Phillip, 1999, p. 192). In this case the 'sex tourist' is servicing the local man rather than the other way around. The power dynamics of male dominance seem well preserved. Oral sex is indeed the practice men have traditionally visited prostituted women to engage in (McLeod, 1982) because of their wives' reluctance. The local men remain in control of the sexual interaction as they would be with any women, tourist or not.

by virtue of male privilege and the construction of male dominant sexuality.

Another very significant difference between 'female' and 'male' sex tourism lies in the degree of harm caused by the behaviour. In relation to male prostitution tourism the harms created are the regular harms that result to women from men's prostitution behaviour whether in the west or in tourist destinations (Farley *et al.*, 1998). Self-mutilation is strongly related to the experience of sexual violence, in childhood, in rape and in prostitution (Jeffreys, 2000b). One British sex tourist to Thailand who spoke to Julia O'Connell Davidson found the self-mutilation engaged in by the women he was prostituting difficult to stomach:

> they cut themselves with a knife. They get drunk and just slash themselves. I find that terrible. When I see a girl, when I'm look-ing to buy her, I always look at her arms to see what she's been doing to herself.
>
> (O'Connell Davidson, 1995, p. 42)

In the case of 'female sex tourism' there does not seem to be evi-dence of the traumatic harm of repeated sexual violation. Indeed researchers agree that because men gain superior masculine status in Caribbean societies amongst their peers according to the number of their sexual conquests, and white women count for more points, beach boys can gain socially from sexual engagement with women tourists (Kempadoo, 1999b). The sex taking place, after all, is the traditional sex of male supremacy, in which the men do the pen-etrating and are not having to disassociate to survive whilst their bodies are used as objects.

In one study of the experience of the women prostituted by male sex tourists in Jamaica (Campbell *et al.*, 1999), the graphic descrip-tions of the violence and danger they are exposed to create a stark contrast with what happens to beach boys, but fit well with accounts of prostitution from the west (Hoigard and Finstad, 1992). Women in the Jamaican study describe as their best experiences those in which they can avoid actually being penetrated, such as being asked to urinate on the client or walk on him in high heels. The worst experiences ranged 'from a client attacking a worker with a machete because of dissatisfaction with the job, to agreeing to have sex with a client who then turned up with six men in a hotel room' (Campbell *et al.*, 1999, p. 140). The women said they never knew whether a client would be dangerous and, as one put it, she was 'full of fear because you don't know what can happen. You always have some fear because you don't know who bad and who good' (ibid., p. 142). Women spoke of having to drink tequila or get stoned on ganja so that they did not have to see the man who was using them. As one woman puts it: 'I love my job but I hate it for the sex. We are talking to a guy, he makes me feel sick but he is paying the price. You have sex with him. It really hurts. It makes your heart get sick too, you know ... He is real ugly, he is real white, he is so soft and you just want to scream' (ibid., p. 150).

The male power which results in the abuse of prostituted women can lead to violence by beach boys against their tourist partners if the relationships progress beyond the duration of the holiday, as many do. In order to include the women within the ranks of sex tourists they are described as having economic power over local men. But this economic power does seem to be the only power they have, and may not necessarily trump the power that the beach boys have over them as a result of their superior position in the gender hierarchy. Sanchez Taylor says that a number of women in her study who had migrated to marry or live with their local boyfriends found themselves in 'extremely abusive relationships' and that when they reported this to the police no action was taken (Sanchez Taylor, 2001, p. 761). Thus, as she points out, 'white privilege can be jeopardized by entry into permanent or semi-permanent' relationships with black men (ibid.). The women's economic and race privilege were only able to hold the men's sex class privilege at bay temporarily, in quite specialized settings.

The differences between the behaviour of male and female sex tourists in terms of its context, meanings and effects are considerable and result from the different positions of men and women under male dominance. Why then do some commentators determinedly place women within the ranks of sex tourists? The decision of whether to include women stems from the different theoretical positions these writers hold on prostitution. Kempadoo uses the inclusion of women as sex tourists to argue that feminist understandings of prostitution as resulting from male dominance are invalid. She explains that the existence of both male and female sex tourists in the Caribbean 'underscores the point that feminist accounts that focus exclusively on the operations of the masculine hegemony to explain prostitution and sex work may not be entirely appropriate' (ibid., p. 57). 'Female sex tourism' allows her to move